CREDIT POWER !

OTHER BOOKS BY JOHN Q. NEWMAN

- *The Heavy Duty New Identity*

- *Understanding U.S. Identity Documents*

- *Be Your Own Dick*

- *Credit Power! Rebuild Your Credit in 90 Days or Less*

- *Handbook of Altered and False Identification*

- *Birth Certificate and Social Security Number Fraud*

with Trent Sands

- *How to Investigate Your Friends, Enemies, and Lovers*

CREDIT POWER !

REBUILD YOUR CREDIT IN 90 DAYS OR LESS

John Q. Newman

Index Publishing Group, Inc.
San Diego, California

CREDIT POWER!

Published by

INDEX PUBLISHING GROUP, Inc.
3368 Governor Drive, Suite 273
San Diego, CA 92122-2936
(619) 455-6100; fax (619) 552-9050
E-mail: ipgbooks@indexbooks.com
Web Site: http://www.electriciti.com/~ipgbooks

Copyright © 1997 by
INDEX PUBLISHING GROUP, Inc.

ISBN 1-56866-131-2 (Quality Paperback)
Library of Congress Card Number 95-81309

Publisher's Cataloging-in-Publication
(Provided by Quality Books, Inc.)

Newman, John Q.
     Credit power: rebuild your credit in 90 days or less! / by John
Q. Newman.-- 1st ed.
     p. cm.
     ISBN: 1-56866-131-2

     1. Consumer credit--United States. 2. Credit ratings--United
States. 3. Credit bureaus--United States.   I. Title.

HG3751.7.N49 1997   332.7'43
                       QB197-4083 8

Cover design: HLE Designs
Text design: in house
Typeset: Cindy Cheek Graphics
Graphics: Cindy Cheek Graphics
Printed and bound by VG Reed & Sons, Indianapolis, IN

Printed in the United States of America
1 2 3 4 5 6 7 8 9

CONTENTS

INTRODUCTION   9

1. THE AMERICAN CREDIT INDUSTRY   11

2. CREDIT GRANTORS   15

    Credit Cards   15
    Installment Loans   18
    Home Mortgage   18

3. THE CREDIT BUREAUS: GATEKEEPERS TO CREDIT   19

    Rejection Of Credit Applications   21
    Credit Reports   22
    Manipulation Of Credit Information   24
    Types Of Credit Reports   25
    Legislative Protection   26

4. LAWS REGULATING THE CREDIT INDUSTRY   27

    Obtaining Copies Of Credit Reports   29
    Credit Clinics   30
    The Problem Of No Credit   31

5. CREDIT PROBLEM 1: INSUFFICIENT CREDIT HISTORY   33

    Secured Bank Cards   34

6. CREDIT PROBLEM 2: NEGATIVE CREDIT INFORMATION   37

    Delinquent Account Data   37
    Disputing Negative Items On Your Credit Report   38
    Filing A Complaint With The FTC   40
    Excessive Inquiries   42
    Taking Legal Action   42
    Dealing Directly With Creditors   43

7. CREDIT PROBLEM 3: NEGATIVE PUBLIC RECORD DATA   47

8. CREDIT PROBLEM 4: CREDIT BUREAU WARNING PROGRAMS   51

    Mail Forwarding And Telephone Answering Services   52
    Name Variations   52
    Social Security Numbers   53
    Disputing Warning Program Data   53

9. FILE SEGREGATION   55

    How File Segregation Works   57
    Now Get A New Credit File   58
    Credit Terms   58
    File Segregation Worksheet   59

10. INSIDER CREDITOR SECRETS: PART ONE   61

11. INSIDER CREDITOR SECRETS: PART TWO   65

   Obtaining Preapproved Credit Cards   66
   Special Qualification Cards   67
   Accumulating Unsecured Credit Lines   68
   Drawbacks To Using Unsecured Credit   69

12. AVOIDING DAMAGE TO YOUR CREDIT REPORT   71

   How Much Credit Can You Afford?   72
   Early Warning Signs Of Credit Problems   72
   Dealing With Credit Problems   73

13. CHECK VERIFICATION SERVICES   77

   How Check Authorization Services Work   78
   Disputing Negative Information   79
   Re-Entering The System   80

14. HOW CREDIT BUREAUS INVADE YOUR PRIVACY   81

15. HOW CREDIT BUREAUS RAPE YOUR CREDIT   85

   Warning Programs   87

16. SPECIAL CREDIT REPORTS   89

17. ONLINE CREDIT INFORMATION   91

18. CONTROVERSIAL SCREENING PROGRAMS   99

   Risk Scores   100

19. NEW DEVELOPMENTS   105

   APPENDIX 1   109

   Equifax Credit Report Legend   109
   Industry Codes   110
   Obtaining Credit Profile   110

   APPENDIX 2   115

   The Fair Credit Reporting Act   116

   APPENDIX 3   127

   Experian (Formerly Known As TRW)   127
   Consumer Credit Report Sample   128
   Credit Report Request Letter   134
   The TRW Credit Profile Report   134
   The TRW Credit Profile Report Messages   136

APPENDIX 4   137

   Credit Repair   138

APPENDIX 5   **139**

    Bank Rate Monitor™   139
    E-Mail Card Fraud? Investigators Checking Pre-Approved Offers   143
    U.S. Code Concerning Credit Reporting Agencies   146
    Secured Credit Card Issuers   148

APPENDIX 6   **151**

    Sample Letters Of Dispute   151

APPENDIX 7   **157**

    DTEC Overview   158

APPENDIX 8   **165**

    ID Report Overview   166
    Finders Overview   170

APPENDIX 9   **177**

    Credit Card Tips   177

APPENDIX 10   **179**

    Victims Of Credit Reporting (VCR)   179
    Credit Scoring   183

APPENDIX 11   **185**

    12 Credit Card Secrets   186

APPENDIX 12   **189**

    Trans Union Credit Report   189

INDEX   **197**

INTRODUCTION

The ability to obtain credit has become a literal necessity in order to survive. People who can't obtain credit find it difficult, if not impossible, to do many basic things in everyday life, for example, rent an automobile, reserve a hotel or motel room, make travel arrangements, even obtain a job. Not so many years ago, all of the above could be done just as easily without credit, but today it is a totally different story.

Renting a car represents a good example. Fifteen years ago most car rental agencies would rent vehicles just as readily to people paying in cash as to those paying with credit cards. If the car rental company's rental requirements were met, usually a minimum age of 25 years, a valid driver's license, and a deposit equal to the amount of the rental, a cash transaction presented no problem. Now, the exact opposite is true. *Not one* of the major national car rental agencies accepts cash deposits. The only exceptions are occasional local franchises that will allow renters known to the company to rent a car with cash. Oddly enough, Hertz Rent-A-Car will allow an individual to qualify for a card to rent cars on a cash basis. The irony is, to get this card, the applicant must have a good credit history.

People who do not have credit, or who have bad credit, are forced to live in a shadow financial world. In that world they pay many times what people with credit do for goods and services, often of lesser quality. Return to the car rental example. In most cities there are small car rental agencies that will rent to people without credit cards. But the price is heavy. The rates charged are much higher than at a regular car rental agency. A deposit of several hundred dollars may be required for a rental of short duration. The vehicles provided often are older and not in the best condition, and finally, a host of restrictions and conditions usually apply.

Landlords also have discovered the utility of checking on an applicant's credit before renting. Ten years ago this was rare. Now it is common, and tenancy applications are designed to allow apartment owners to easily check the credit histories of applicants. The same is true of employers. Most people don't realize that lack of credit, or a bad credit history, can make it very difficult to find a job.

As you can see, a person who can't obtain credit is "at risk" in society. He or she may not be able to find employment—or even a place to live. Two types of individuals are "at risk." The first is the person who has no credit at all. People without credit can rectify the situation easily by following the correct steps. However, they can just as easily make their problem worse if they are not careful.

The second type of person at risk is the one with bad credit. Bad credit is very common. Prior recessions caused hundreds of thousands of people to lose jobs that were once secure and to later suffer credit problems as a result.

Even people who pay their bills on time can suffer from "bad credit." Errors in credit bureau files cause many thousands of people to be denied credit each day. For this reason, anyone who doesn't know his or her credit standing is potentially at risk.

The good news is that almost any bad credit problem can be corrected by following the proper procedure.

Credit Power! examines all aspects of the credit industry. It takes a detailed look at the credit bureaus, credit card issuers, banks, and finance companies, and how they all fit together. The book then looks at common credit problems and shows how they can be solved by following proper procedures.

Good credit is as necessary to life today as clean air and water. *Credit Power!* shows you how to obtain good credit no matter what your present situation.

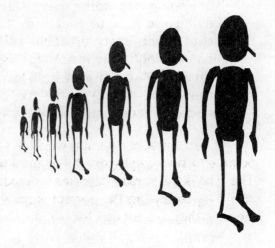

CHAPTER 1

THE AMERICAN CREDIT INDUSTRY

The granting of credit is an industry, just like any other. Stripped to its essentials, the credit industry allows individuals to purchase what they want or need now with *someone else's money*. The credit industry makes its profits through interest charges and service fees. To ensure that profits are made, the grantors of credit seek to reduce the amount of "risk" associated with each borrower. However, there is always *some* element of risk, no matter how small, with every borrower. To reduce this risk, credit grantors use certain criteria to qualify customers for loans, including income, years on a job, number of dependents, a telephone in the home, and the most important criterion of all—**the applicant's past history of paying credit obligations.**

The best illustration of the credit industry in action is to look at a typical credit transaction from start to finish.

On a Saturday afternoon, a couple in their early 30s are shopping for some new furniture. At a particular store they find a living room suite that they like for $1,500. Our couple doesn't have that much cash available and they tell the salesperson as much. The salesperson says not to worry because the store offers "instant financing" on the store's own credit card. The couple is directed to the credit office to see the credit manager. At this point, our couple become "credit applicants" in the credit industry.

The first step will be for the couple to fill out a credit application. This form will ask for a number of details about their lives. Personal identifying information will be requested. This usually consists of full name, date of birth, Social Security Number, and home address and telephone number. The next section normally asks for employment details with an emphasis on length of time with the present employer and the position held. The last section asks about financial and credit data. The applicant's gross annual income will be requested, along with information on bank accounts and previous creditors.

Once the application has been completed, it will be scored by the credit manager. This scoring process ensures that the applicants meet the minimum lending criteria of the lender. We should digress at this point to make a clarification. Most stores that offer financing or a store credit card no longer actually issue the credit themselves. Most establishments have contracted with an outside credit grantor to open and maintain the credit accounts. This outside firm may be a bank, or just as often a finance company, and may be located thousands of miles away from the actual store. If the applicants pass the scoring hurdle, the next step is for the information on the in-store application to be sent, via computer or fax machine, to the new account processing department of the credit grantor. When the information arrives, the first step will be to pull a credit history or credit report on the applicants from one of the credit bureaus. Credit bureaus act as gatekeepers in the credit industry.

The report from the credit bureau tells the credit grantor two key facts. The first is whether the applicant pays his or her bills on time. This is by far the most important determining factor about the applicant. Credit grantors firmly believe that people are creatures of habit and do not change much over time. Creditors have learned from experience that people who have paid their bills on time in the past are likely to do so in the future.

The second important fact the credit report tells the lender is whether the credit applicant is amassing too much debt relative to his or her income. If this is indeed the case, the credit grantor will see this as a warning sign of a possible future default. This type of behavior will be reflected on the credit report by the existence of numerous accounts, typically credit cards, that are at or near the credit limit with only minimum monthly payments being made on the outstanding balance.

As you can see, the credit grantor does a very complex dance, trying to balance risk against the possibility of opening a new account that may provide thousands of dollars of profit in interest charges over the next few years. This judgment call on who to accept and who to reject is called "*credit culture.*" Every creditor has a different credit culture. What is an acceptable risk to one is an unacceptable risk to another. This will be discussed in more detail later, but for now assume that our couple fits the credit culture of our furniture store lender.

The new accounts person will then assign an account number to the application and, most importantly, set a credit limit on the account. This limit will either be a standard amount for all new accounts or may be based on the applicant's income. Once this account set-up has been done, the account number and credit limit will be faxed or modemed back to the credit manager in the store. Our couple is then able to complete their purchase. In two to three weeks they will also receive their new furniture store credit card from the lender's processing facility.

This brief example has illustrated all of the major players in the credit industry—the merchant, the credit grantor, the credit bureau, and, of course, the all important credit applicant. Before dealing with specific credit problems, we need to take a careful look at how credit grantors and credit bureaus operate. There is a lot of confusion and many misconceptions over the roles of both of these players in the credit industry. Let's look first at the credit grantors.

CHAPTER 2

CREDIT GRANTORS

A credit grantor, or creditor for short, can be defined as any individual or institution that will provide someone with goods or services *now* in return for the promise of payment *later*. By this definition, the list of credit grantors includes the telephone companies and local gas and electric utilities, as well as more traditional creditors like banks and finance companies.

The most visible form of credit today is the credit card, and we will begin with this form of credit because it is the cause of the vast majority of credit problems.

CREDIT CARDS

Credit cards can be divided into three main types. The first is the bank credit card. There are three brands—Visa, MasterCard, and Discover. The second type of credit cards are travel and entertainment cards. The most popular brands are American Express and Diner's Club. The last type of credit card is the private issue card. The best examples of these are department store and oil company cards. Although all three types are credit cards, there are many important differences between them. Let's look at the bank credit cards first.

BANK CREDIT CARDS

The first misconception about bank credit cards is that they are issued by the Visa and MasterCard organizations. The fact is that these cards are issued by **individual financial institutions**. The bank card is a remarkable invention. A bank card allows the holder to purchase goods and services at any number of businesses and then pay the particular card issuer later. When a consumer makes a bank card transaction, the bank that issued the card pays the merchant the amount of the sale less a small processing fee. The sale amount is then billed to the cardholder's account.

Visa and MasterCard are what are known as **Interbank Associations**. A bank pays a fee to join each group and in return is allowed to issue credit cards bearing the logo of the respective group. Many banks are now members of both organizations. What does a bank gain by belonging? Acceptance of its credit cards. When an individual uses a bank card at a merchant, the merchant could care less what bank issued the card. The merchant just cares that the card is a Visa or MasterCard. This guarantees he will be paid.

The interbank groups decide on the **account numbering system** for each bank. On a Visa or MasterCard, the first four or six digits identify to the computer which bank issued the card. The interbank groups also maintain the **worldwide authorization system** for the cards. This global system is what allows you to use a bankcard issued by your local bank in Japan or Germany as easily as you would use it at home.

Each issuing bank sets its own policies on credit qualifications and credit limits. It is possible to qualify for a bank card at one bank and be rejected at another.

Bank cards offer what is known as **revolving credit**. This means that a purchase can "revolve" each month with the cardholder only having to pay a minimum monthly payment. This is different than an installment loan where a fixed amount must be paid each month to pay off the loan in a certain time period. A bank card holder can pay any amount between the minimum payment due, to the full balance outstanding. Each issuing bank decides the minimum payment and interest rates charged on outstanding balances.

Bank cards come in **two different levels**. The first is the "classic" or regular variety Visa or MasterCard. These cards generally have credit limits up to $3,000 and usually carry an annual fee in the $15 range. The bank card issuers also issue "premier" versions of their bank cards. These upscale versions usually have credit limits starting at a minimum of $5,000. The premier versions also include enhancements such as rental car collision insurance and expedited card replacement in case the holder loses the card. In general, credit standards are higher for these cards.

The other bank card brand is the Discover card. The Discover card operates much like a Visa or MasterCard. The Discover card was launched in the mid 1980s by Sears Corporation.

Sears wanted to tap into the bank card industry and purchased a bank to issue the cards. The Discover card is accepted at many merchants in the United States but not by many outside the country.

One primary difference between bank cards and other types of credit cards is that bank credit cards can be used for cash advances at banks and automated teller machines. Cash advances are billed against the cardholder's credit limit just as a purchase is. Cash advances incur an added transaction fee, usually 2%, of the amount taken. There is no "grace period" on cash advances, and interest begins accruing at once on the advance.

TRAVEL AND ENTERTAINMENT CARDS

Travel and entertainment cards serve a slightly different segment of the public. They are more correctly called **charge cards**. The bill must be paid in full when it arrives. Travel and entertainment cards were originally intended for businessmen who needed to charge airline tickets, rental cars, hotel stays, and client entertainment. These cards did not have an assigned credit limit because most of the charges would be reimbursed by the employee's company. American Express makes note of the lack of a preset credit limit in its advertising.

Travel and entertainment cards are now held by millions more than just businessmen. This is due to heavy marketing efforts by the card issuers to the general public and also by the card issuers' efforts to sign up merchants outside the traditional traveling businessmen groups. These cards can now be used at the same number of locations as bank cards. The credit qualifications for travel and entertainment cards are higher than for bank cards. Advertising for these cards may imply that there is no credit limit, but as we will see later, this is not entirely true.

PROPRIETARY CARDS

Proprietary cards are the last type of credit card. These encompass the various department store and gasoline company cards. The primary difference between these cards and other types of credit cards is that proprietary cards usually can be used only at the business named on the front. There are a few exceptions to this. For example, a few department store credit cards can be used at certain auto rental agencies. Oil companies and department stores look at these cards as a way to build customer loyalty and increase sales. As mentioned earlier, most department stores no longer actually issue the credit on their cards. The cards are issued by an outside bank or finance company, and it is this bank that carries the account. The stores prefer it this way because they get the benefit of credit sales without having to maintain a credit and collections department and, most importantly, they avoid the financial burden of defaulted accounts.

PORTABLE LOANS

The one aspect that all credit cards have in common is that they are in effect a portable loan. Every time a credit card is used, the card issuer in effect is making an immediate loan to the cardholder to cover the purchase. Credit cards have revolutionized our way of life. A person can take a trip around the world easily if he or she has a credit card. If cash is needed, a quick trip to a bank or automated teller machine will provide it. There is very little a person cannot purchase with a credit card. Credit cards also allow the holder to establish creditworthiness immediately. A credit card is prima facie evidence that the individual presenting it is creditworthy.

INSTALLMENT LOANS

Installment loans are the next largest segment of the credit industry. These can be either secured or unsecured, and can cover almost any amount. An installment loan differs from a credit card loan in that it is for a fixed amount and a fixed term. These terms are determined at the outset of the loan. A good example of such a credit transaction is an automobile loan.

AUTOMOBILE LOAN

An automobile loan is a secured, fixed-term, installment loan. When the loan is made, the bank or finance company takes the title of the vehicle until the loan is paid off. The loan itself will be from 12 to 60 months duration, with 48 months being the most popular. The interest rate and monthly payment are determined at the outset of the loan. When the loan is paid off, the title is returned to the borrower. Automobile loans can be obtained from banks and credit unions as well as from dealer financing. When a dealer finances a new car, the actual lender is usually the finance subsidiary of one of the major automobile companies. The finance company pays the dealer and puts the loan on its books. The finance subsidiary then pays the parent company profits on the loans through stock dividends and bond interest payments.

HOME MORTGAGE

The last type of credit is the home mortgage. This is really just a specialized type of secured installment loan, with the property being used as collateral. Mortgage loan companies take special steps in assessing a potential borrower because of the size of the loan.

As we saw in our example of the couple applying for a loan to purchase furniture, the credit bureaus play a key role in the credit industry. Credit bureaus do not grant or deny credit, but their files determine whom the credit industry will do business with and who it will avoid.

CHAPTER 3

THE CREDIT BUREAUS: GATEKEEPERS TO CREDIT

Credit bureaus are truly the gatekeepers to the world of credit. The files a credit bureau maintains will determine whether or not credit applicants will be approved or denied. Credit bureaus traffic in information, particularly information on how consumers pay their bills. Credit bureaus voraciously amass this data from credit grantors and other sources.

There are three main providers of consumer credit data in the United States. These are: **Experian (formerly TRW)**; (Appendix 3), **Trans Union Corporation** (Appendix 12), and **Equifax** (Appendix 1). See p.29–30 for contact information. Nearly every local credit bureau in the United states is either owned by or affiliated with these three giants, often called "the big three." Credit bureaus have radically altered the way credit is granted in the United States. To illustrate this, compare the way the same couple applying for credit in a furniture store in the last chapter would have obtained credit 25 years earlier in the late 1960s.

> The couple would still have filled out the application. If it had been a Saturday afternoon, the credit manager would have told the couple that a decision could not be made until Monday. Instead of just a brief chat with the couple, the credit manager would have talked in more detail with them. He would want to know about the couple's employment and how they liked their jobs and the area. He would want to know someone, or maybe two people, who would act as a reference for the couple. He would probably even ask if they had children or were planning them in the future. In short, he would want to develop a "feel" for whether these people were a good credit risk.
>
> On the following Monday morning, the credit manager would telephone the couple's employers and ask about the applicants. He would then call the couple's bank to see if they kept their accounts in order. Finally, he would call any other creditors the couple had listed, as well as the personal references. If all of this checked out, the credit would be issued. If the local credit bureau was contacted, it was only to make sure that the couple was not listed in their files of deadbeats.

The key point is that credit bureaus have all but eliminated the process of direct reference checking by credit grantors. Almost all creditors now rely on credit bureau files to verify what is on an applicant's credit request. This is exactly how the credit bureaus want it. The credit bureau industry has transformed itself from a repository of names of people who did not pay their bills into a database of *everyone* who has any type of credit.

This was done by purchasing local credit bureaus outright or by having them sign affiliation agreements with the corporate bureau. These agreements allow the local bureaus to have access to the files of the larger bureau in exchange for sharing their files with it. The local bureaus readily agreed to this trading situation because the large corporations had computerized files. At that time, the late 1960s and early 1970s, computers were expensive and centered around mainframes that only larger businesses could afford. Later, the big bureaus allowed the small local bureaus to have remote terminal access to their mainframes.

The second front of the credit bureau battle was being fought with the credit grantors themselves. Each credit report that a credit grantor orders from a credit bureau costs money.

In the late 1960s, many credit grantors did not use credit reports because they did their own reference checking. The credit bureaus had to convince credit grantors to do away with this and rely on the credit bureau report as the sole verification of the application data.

To do this, the credit bureaus had to convince the credit grantors that their files were comprehensive. The first step toward this goal was to get as many creditors as possible to report the status of all their accounts to the credit bureau, to no longer send just the bad accounts that had been written off, but also the accounts in good standing. The second step was to get information on consumers from as many places as possible. This meant getting information from local courthouses on liens and judgments as well as following who had declared bankruptcy and checking to see who had outstanding tax liens. All of this information would be fed into the credit bureaus' mainframe, searching for "hits" or matches against consumers already in the file.

The credit bureaus' pitch to the credit grantors was strong. The credit bureau would know if John Q. Customer had been a deadbeat in another state. Local reference checking would not reveal this. A credit bureau report on a consumer would be faster, more accurate, and a lot less expensive than doing it yourself. Losses could be reduced and money saved by getting rid of application-processing personnel. Slowly but surely nearly every creditor came to rely only on credit reports to verify an application.

REJECTION OF CREDIT APPLICATIONS

It is the use of a credit report that allows a store in Oregon to solicit customers in California. Credit bureau reports allow a small bank in Ohio to issue credit cards to people living in Maine. Credit grantors like the credit bureau system because it allows them to extend credit anywhere in the nation relatively cheaply. However, this system is far from perfect, and for all of its benefits, can cause consumers many problems. One of these problems is that *people who do not yet have a credit history may find it impossible to get credit*. Let's look at a typical example.

Mary Roberts is 24 years old. She is a professional engineer, out of college for about a year. She has a good job, has lived at the same apartment for nearly two years, makes a good income, and has both a checking and savings account in good standing. She has very little debt and makes $30,000 per year. By any criterion, she would be an excellent credit risk. One day Mary sees a credit card application at her bank and decides to apply for a Visa card. She assumes she will get the card. Three weeks later she is shocked when she gets a letter of rejection. The reason given? Insufficient credit history. Mary does not understand why the bank did not consider her job, her salary, or even the fact that she is a good customer. The reason they didn't is because the credit bureau has told them these facts are not relevant.

A distinction needs to be made clear between passing a credit scoring system and having an acceptable credit report. Mary's job and income allowed her to pass the bank's scoring system easily. The scoring system allows the bank to weed out people who do not fit a lender's credit culture. Each credit report ordered costs the lender money, so the scoring system eliminates wasting large sums of money spent on ordering credit reports on people who will be rejected.

Insufficient credit history is one of the most common credit problems caused by the total reliance of credit bureaus and lenders on bureau reports for application verification. Specific solutions to this credit problem and others will be discussed in later chapters. First we need to examine what goes on in a credit report and how the bureau gets its information.

CREDIT REPORTS

A credit report contains four general types of information. The first type of data is **personal identifying information**. This information includes your full name, date of birth, Social Security Number, and address. This information allows the credit bureau computer to locate the credit report that belongs to you and you alone. Later, we will see that this proper matchup is not always the case and can be a source of credit problems.

The next information on the credit report is **employment and financial data**. This information consists of the name of the applicant's employer, the employer's address, and the length of time at the job. The financial data usually is limited to the amount of salary. This section is frequently incomplete on credit reports.

The next section contains the actual **credit history**. This is the most important section of the credit report. The credit history section contains entries for each credit account. A complete entry occupies one line across the report. The entry will contain the following information:

Name of Creditor	Account Number
Account Balance	Account Credit Limit
Minimum Payment Due	Payment History Rating

Most of these items are self-explanatory. The credit report legends in Appendix 1 illustrate different credit report formats and decode the shorthand used. The most important item is the *payment history rating*. This rating is often the first item a creditor looks at. Payment history ratings can rank from a **zero (0)** to a **nine (9)**. A **zero** indicates that the account is too new to rate, a **9** indicates that the account had to be written off and sent to a collection agency.

A **1** by each account listed is the best rating to have. It indicates that the individual pays on time. A person with all **1**s on his or her credit history will in general be able to get loans on the most favorable terms.

A **2** indicates that the person is a little slow in paying bills. This person is usually one payment cycle late, or 30 days. This individual is still an okay risk, but has what is known in the industry as "slow credit." A **3** also indicates slow credit, but because a **3** indicates up to 60 days late on payment, this person is a much higher risk than an individual with a **2** rating.

Most creditors will not extend credit to people who have accounts on their credit history with ratings of **4** through **9**. Experience has taught creditors that most people who have **4**s on their credit reports will deteriorate into a total charge-off situation a few months later. On the other hand, some creditors actively cultivate what is known as the "slow credit" market of borrowers who have lots of **2**s and the occasional **3** on their credit report. These creditors make profits through high interest charges and careful monitoring of these accounts.

Payment histories will be reported on each account for a minimum of the last year. This is a very important point to consider. If a consumer was two months late on a payment five months ago, this fact will remain on the credit report even though the last four payments have been made on time. This fact allows a credit report to provide a glimpse of how a consumer *pays his or her bills over time*—not a one-shot glance.

The next section of the credit report contains what is known as **public record information**. This information is gathered primarily from local county courthouse records and the Federal Bankruptcy Court. Credit bureaus purchase extracts from county clerks that provide summaries of all liens and judgments filed against individuals the previous week. Often the credit bureau will contract with an outside vendor to provide this service. Once the information is gathered, it is matched against existing files in credit bureau computers. A match will result in a brief description of the judgment and where it was filed being added to the consumer's credit report.

As an example, let us assume that a $5,000 judgment is filed by a housing contractor against a credit applicant who did not pay him for a job. The details of this filing will show up on the public record section of the credit report. Even if the judgment is later dismissed, *it will still show up* on the credit report.

The erroneous reporting of public record items on credit reports is one of the biggest causes of credit problems for consumers. The plaintiff, the one who files the suit, will often have his or her credit tarnished because the credit bureau will report the lawsuit on both the credit report of the *plaintiff* and the *defendant*. The report will not state who was the plaintiff and who was the defendant.

The last part of the credit report lists everyone who has requested the person's credit report for the last six months. This section is called the **inquiry section**. Excessive inquiries can cause a credit problem in and of themselves. Consider the earlier example of the single female engineer. If she continues applying for credit cards after she was turned down the first time, she will probably be rejected each additional time she applies for a credit card. All of the rejections will be listed on her credit report. After each subsequent rejection, it will become even more difficult for her to establish credit. Each later creditor will wonder why they should be the one to extend credit when the other creditors have rejected her.

MANIPULATION OF CREDIT INFORMATION

Credit bureaus no longer just record credit information, they also *manipulate it*. Credit bureaus have convinced creditors they are doing their jobs via two avenues. The first is by collecting as much negative information on credit applicants as possible.

NEGATIVE INFORMATION

Consider the many ways negative credit information can get on a credit report. Each creditor an individual has can report negative information to the bureau. Public record information is also amassed by the bureaus, and this can cover a wide spectrum. Local judgments and liens can be recorded, as well as judgments obtained by state, county, and Federal government agencies such as the IRS. On some specialized credit reports, criminal conviction information is also included. These specialized reports will be detailed later. And remember, an unknown person can tarnish your credit report just by filing a frivolous lawsuit against you.

"ENHANCED" REPORTS

Negative data also can get on your credit report via a second avenue credit bureaus use to "enhance" the value of their reports to creditors. For each "enhancement" a creditor orders, an additional charge is paid to the credit bureau. Examples of such enhancements are the many different **warning programs** credit bureaus use to try and trip up people who are trying to leave behind a bad credit history. Let's look at a few of them.

One of these programs flashes a warning across the face of the credit report if the **Social Security Number used is different than the one already in the system**. People trying to leave behind a poor credit history often give a different Social Security Number than their real one. But this warning system can cause problems for people who make an honest mistake on a credit application, or if a clerical error is made on the computer by the data entry clerk. If one digit in the applicant's Social Security Number is accidentally transposed, this warning will be flashed across the screen and will end up on the credit report.

Another source of problems are the credit bureau warning programs designed to **detect a credit applicant who is using an alias**. Some people attempt to start a fresh credit history by changing their name slightly and leaving everything else the same. Needless to say, this doesn't work, and the credit bureau's warning program will flash "AKA" and the name used previously. AKA is police jargon for "Also Known As."

You have to be very careful about how your name is recorded. If you last applied for credit as Robert F. Simmons Jr., and on the next credit application you apply as Bob F. Simmons, the credit bureau computer will also flash an "AKA" warning.

Another enhancement offered by credit bureaus is a **rating of a particular credit history** to indicate if the credit applicant is headed for credit trouble in the future even if all of his or her current bills are being paid on time. These warnings take one of two forms.

First, a credit bureau calculates your total available credit on all unsecured revolving credit—credit cards and unsecured lines of personal credit—and then calculates the total balance outstanding. It divides the balance outstanding by the amount of credit available and converts this into a percentage.

For example, an applicant has $10,000 available in credit cards and a total credit card debt of $6,000; outstanding, this translates to a figure of 60%. Some credit bureaus provide guidelines on how this should be interpreted by the creditor. For example, some say that when this figure hits 80% the credit applicant is **entering the danger zone** and no further credit should be extended.

Second, another more sophisticated system is supposed to identify customers who are a **bankruptcy or total charge-off risk**. This program tracks variables such as customer income, total available credit, amount of credit used, and how quickly a credit applicant goes through lines of credit. This is all boiled down into a score that is supposed to give the relative chances of customer default.

Both of these systems can cause problems for creditworthy people. Consider the case of a man who is unemployed for five months and is forced to use credit card cash advances to augment his unemployment insurance payments for living expenses. These systems could easily show him to be a bankruptcy risk because his debt cloud will increase quickly over a short period of time. If one of his creditors pulls a new credit history, they may cancel an existing line of credit that is badly needed because they see a bankruptcy risk on the credit report.

Another warning program deals with people who have a lot of **inquiries in a short period of time** on their credit report If more than four credit inquiries are made within a six-month period, a warning will be flashed across the credit report saying that excessive credit inquiries have been made. Many creditors will reject an application for credit on this basis alone.

It may seem odd that credit bureaus are so involved in trying to have people *denied* credit. It must be understood that credit bureaus are **not in the business of extending credit**. The business of the credit bureaus is to *sell credit reports*. The credit bureau could care less if eight out of ten consumers were denied credit based on the information contained in their files. All they care about is selling credit histories to each and every creditor. This is how they make their money. Each day nearly *a million* credit reports change hands. This is big business.

TYPES OF CREDIT REPORTS

There are two types of credit reports: the **standard consumer credit report** and the **investigative credit report**. Most people are the subject of the standard consumer credit report, which is the type that is pulled for most consumer loans. The investigative credit report is pulled for very large loans, and frequently for employment purposes. We need to look at the latter use of credit reports in pre-employment screening.

INVESTIGATIVE REPORTS

The Fair Credit Reporting Act allows employers to pull credit reports on job applicants. This law is discussed in detail in the next chapter. What we want to establish here is the fact that employers can easily request a copy of a job applicant's credit history. The potential employment need not have anything to do with money handling or financial management for a credit report to be pulled.

Investigative reports are commonly used in connection with employment and for the purchase of large insurance policies. Such a report will start with the credit history that is on an ordinary credit report and then adds additional information.

The credit bureau will check for a **criminal record**. This will be done via checking at the local courthouses in the counties of all of the applicant's previous residences. If the subject has lived in a state that allows outsider access to its central crime computer, a check will be made at this level for a criminal record.

The next part of the investigative report involves confirming **employment and salary details at all former employers**. Usually, creditors accept salary information without verification, and most such information on standard credit reports is unverified. It is taken directly from the application. But an investigative credit report often verifies, in writing, the credit applicant's salary and job details.

Finally, an investigative credit report often involves having a **field investigator** call or contact in person the references and neighbors of the credit applicant. The field investigator attempts to ascertain the stability and reliability of the applicant. As one might suspect, these reports are subject to a high degree of unreliability. A cranky neighbor can destroy an individual's job prospects.

LEGISLATIVE PROTECTION

The Fair Credit Reporting Act requires that an individual be notified any time a credit report is pulled in regard to the extension of credit or in connection with a job or insurance application. The Fair Credit Reporting Act is one of the most powerful tools in the hands of consumers who have been wronged by credit bureaus. This law, along with the companion Fair Credit Act, regulates the credit industry. To effectively combat credit problems, *consumers need to understand these laws.*

CHAPTER 4

LAWS REGULATING THE CREDIT INDUSTRY

The Fair Credit Reporting Act is the Federal law passed by Congress in 1970 that sets certain minimum standards for credit grantors to follow in conducting their business. This law was designed to eliminate the widespread credit abuses that were very common in the 1960s. These abuses included, but were not limited to, failure to disclose the true interest rate being charged, hidden fees and service charges, and arbitrary default policies. Much of the fine print that accompanies credit cards and other loans is a result of this law. This is also the law that outlawed racial discrimination by credit grantors and required creditors to make credit available to all creditworthy people on an equal basis.

The Fair Credit Reporting Act governs the activities of the credit reporting industry—the credit bureaus. The legacy of abuses by credit bureaus led to passage of this law. It gives credit consumers specific rights with regard to information contained in credit bureau reports. The full text of the Fair Credit Reporting Act is given in Appendix 2 and I strongly recommend you read it carefully. It also should be noted that these Federal laws do not prohibit individual states from enacting consumer legislation that has stronger protection than the Federal laws—and many have.

Examples of stronger state laws are those in some states that set maximum annual interest rates on credit accounts or that outlaw penalty fees for being over the credit limit. A close look at the information panel on a typical credit card application will list a number of different interest rates and annual fee levels. These variations are due to different state laws.

Examples of state laws that affect credit bureaus are those in many states that allow a consumer who has been wronged by a credit bureau to sue in Small Claims Court or County Court under the particular state counterpart to the Federal Fair Credit Reporting Act. States that have particularly strong consumer protection legislation, like California, allow people who have been wronged by credit bureaus to collect substantial penalties.

The Fair Credit Reporting Act provides a number of beneficial protections for consumers. One of the most important parts of the law says that the credit bureaus must supply free of charge a credit report to anyone who is rejected on a credit application because of information contained in the particular credit bureau's files.

Another obligation the law imposes on credit bureaus is investigation of consumer complaints within a reasonable period of time. The credit bureau can refuse to investigate a claim only if it is "frivolous." The definition of "frivolous" is subject to interpretation. Most credit bureau problems are solved by using this part of the act. In short, the law requires that an item must be removed from a credit report the first time the credit bureau cannot verify the entry with the creditor within a reasonable time.

The Federal Trade Commission, or FTC for short, administers compliance with the Federal law. Most consumers can solve most credit problems on their own without retaining a lawyer or high-priced credit clinic by using the provisions of the law. In the next few chapters we will look at the solutions to different types of credit problems.

The Fair Credit Reporting Act also sets limits on how long negative information can be reported on a consumer's credit report. Most negative information must be removed after seven years. Bankruptcy can be reported for up to ten years. There are some exceptions to these rules.

If a credit report is pulled on an applicant who earns or who has applied for a job that pays more than $20,000 per year, negative information can be reported essentially forever. The same is true when the credit report is requested for an extension of credit in excess of $50,000. These exceptions were made to give creditors and employers added security when making very large loans or when offering employment at relatively high salaries.

The drafters of the Fair Credit Reporting Act could not have conceived at the time that the average home mortgage in the late 1990s would greatly exceed $50,000 and that a salary of $20,000 would be inadequate to support a family.

Fortunately, most creditors and employers request only the garden variety credit report when extending credit or offering employment. The only cases where the special reports are ordered are for jobs with large financial or managerial responsibility, and the special case of mortgage loans, which we will examine later.

There are five main bad credit problems. Almost any credit problem can be reduced to a combination of the following:

- **Insufficient Credit History**
- **Excessive Credit Inquiries**
- **Negative Credit History Information**
- **Negative Public Record Information**
- **Credit Bureau Warning Programs**

OBTAINING COPIES OF CREDIT REPORTS

The solution to *any* credit problem begins with the consumer obtaining a copy of his or her credit report. **A copy of the report must be obtained from all three main credit bureaus**. This is a vital step. Correcting a credit problem at one credit bureau will have no bearing on the credit reports maintained on the same consumer at the other two bureaus. The credit bureaus compete with each other. Through various enticements and aggressive pricing, they attempt to convince each creditor to select their bureau over the competition. Having clean credit at all three credit bureaus allows you to apply for credit with confidence from any creditor.

You can obtain your credit report from each major bureau by contacting them at the customer service addresses listed here, or by looking in your telephone book Yellow Pages under the heading of "Credit Reporting Agencies." If you have been turned down for credit, a copy of the rejection letter will allow you to obtain a free copy of your report from the credit bureau consulted by the creditor. The national addresses for credit report requests are:

Experian (formerly TRW)
P.O. Box 949
Allen TX 75013-0949
(800) 643-3334
(214) 390-9191
http://www.experian.com

Trans Union Corporation
Consumer Disclosure Center
P.O. Box 390
Springfield PA 19064-0390
(800) 916-8800
(800) 682-7654
(714) 680-7292
http://www.tuc.com

Equifax
P.O. Box 740241
Atlanta GA 30374-0241
(800) 685-1111
(770) 612-3200
(800) 548-4548 residents of Georgia, Vermont, or Massachusetts
(800) 233-7654 residents of Maryland
Order online at http://www.equifax.com/consumer/consumer.html

If you write to obtain a copy of your credit report, you will need to provide sufficient information in your letter to allow the concerned credit bureau to positively identify your individual report. Identifying information consisting of your **full name**, **birthdate**, and **Social Security Number** must be furnished. A sample credit report request letter is included in Appendix 3. Use this as your model. The letter should be neatly typed or handwritten. Expect to receive your credit report in about three weeks.

CREDIT CLINICS

Before we look at the solutions to specific credit problems, we need to be aware of one type of credit industry business that should be avoided. Newspapers all over the country, radio and television stations, advertise companies that guarantee they can clean up your credit. These firms make it sound as if they have access to secret insider methods unknown to an ordinary consumer. These claims are patently false, and in fact, *dealing with a credit clinic can sometimes make your situation worse.*

All credit clinics (sometimes known as **credit repair agencies**) make use of the portion of the Fair Credit Reporting Act that requires credit bureaus to investigate consumer complaints of inaccurate information in credit bureau files. The law also states that the first time the credit bureau is unable to verify a particular entry on a credit report, the offending item must be removed. This must occur within a reasonable period of time, which is customarily accepted to be four to six weeks.

Credit clinics will **dispute everything** on the credit history, often using form letters for all correspondence with the credit bureau. Five years ago these agencies often were quite successful in cleaning up bad credit files. This is no longer the case. Credit clinics hit the credit bureaus with so many challenges that the bureaus wised up and now routinely reject requests for verification of credit history information that originate from credit clinics. As mentioned earlier, the Fair Credit Reporting Act allows credit bureaus to refuse to investigate verification requests that are deemed to be frivolous.

If the credit clinic is met with a rejection from all three major credit bureaus, some will then offer another solution to the customer. This solution involves the creation of **a brand new credit file**. Depending on how this is done, it can be outright illegal. The bottom line is that the consumer will pay a credit clinic hundreds of dollars for a service that can be accomplished on his or her own easier, cheaper, and more effectively. The other consideration to keep in mind is that in most states there is no regulation of credit repair agencies. You could be ripped off and have no recourse.

THE PROBLEM OF NO CREDIT

The easiest credit problem to solve is that of the person who has no credit at all. The person has no bad credit, but also has no good credit. We will begin with this scenario in our chapters on solving specific credit problems.

A useful Internet resource for warnings about credit repair agencies (and credit repair in general) can be found at Credit Repair Kits site (`http://amdream.com/credit/warning.htm`). A sample screen capture is in Appendix 4.

CHAPTER 5

CREDIT PROBLEM 1: INSUFFICIENT CREDIT HISTORY

The problem of a lack of credit history may be compared to an airline crew making its first flight. If the captain were to announce to the passengers that this was the first flight of the crew since leaving flight school, how many of the passengers would want to remain on board? Very few, probably. Creditors are the same way when dealing with someone who is new to the world of credit. *No creditor wants to be your first creditor*. This explains why the first time a person applies for credit from most creditors, the application is invariably rejected. A person with no credit history needs to seek out creditors that want to lend to stable people who have no past credit record.

These creditors generally charge a higher interest rate and lend a lesser amount than creditors catering to people with established credit records. This is due to the fact that borrowers without existing credit records are considered high-risk loans. They are considered to be high risk until they have established themselves on one account. One of the easiest ways to get around the insufficient credit history problem is through a secured bank credit card program.

SECURED BANK CARDS

A secured bank credit card works and looks just like its unsecured counterpart. The only difference is that the secured credit card has a deposit amount equal to the credit limit backing it up. The lender feels secure in the knowledge that if for some reason the cardholder cannot make his payments, they can be made by the bank from the security deposit. The deposit money goes into an interest-bearing savings account that is signed over to the bank for as long as the credit card is held by the consumer.

QUALIFICATIONS FOR SECURED CARDS

To qualify for most secured credit card programs, an applicant will need to meet the following criteria:

> A listed home telephone number
>
> Verifiable employment
>
> No current serious credit problems
>
> An income of at least $10,000 per year

A secured card issuer will do what creditors used to do. They will call your employer and verify directly that you work where you say you do. They will call your bank and make sure your checking and savings accounts are in order. They will pull a credit report to make sure you are not in any current credit problems that could affect their chances of being repaid. There is much flexibility on what secured credit card issuers consider to be a disqualifying credit problem.

Most secured card vendors will not issue a card to someone who is still going through bankruptcy. The deposit used to secure the account potentially could be taken by the bankruptcy court to be paid out to current creditors. A person who has been discharged from bankruptcy will almost always be accepted because this person's obligations have all been eliminated and another bankruptcy petition cannot be filed for a number of years.

SHOPPING FOR SECURED BANK CARDS

One must shop carefully for a secured credit card bank. Some of the offers are no more than carefully designed ripoffs. When dealing with a secured credit card issuer, you should never have to pay a fee for the application. The application form should also state which bank is the issuer of the card. There are a lot of scams in the secured credit card market, and one of the more popular ones involves applications.

The **application scam** usually involves an unsolicited letter from a generic "Bankcard Center" arriving in the mail. The application will say that you have been preselected or pre-approved to apply for a bank credit card. The application will quite short, not identify a specific issuing bank, and require a fee of around $20 to be returned with the application. Once the application has been returned to the so-called bankcard center, the applicant is sent the *real* application from a secured card issuing bank. Your $20 has been wasted. You should only complete secured card applications that identify the bank that will issue the credit card.

A legitimate secured card bank will require you to pay a processing fee along with a deposit. Most secured card issuers have you pay the processing fee when you submit the application, and you only submit the deposit after credit approval has been granted. If your application is rejected, the processing fee will be returned. More banks are getting into this market all of the time, and an organization called Bankcard Holders of America publishes an up-to-the-minute listing of these issuers for a small fee. Their address is:

Bankcard Holders of America
524 Branch Drive
Salem, VA 24153
(703) 389-5445

If you are online, you can also obtain a comprehensive listing of current secured credit card issuers from Bank Rate™ Monitor (http://www.bankrate.com). A sample screen capture from their site is in Appendix 5.

There are additional considerations when choosing a secured card bank. Such a card is a means to an end. The secured credit card issuer should be willing to convert your account to unsecured status after a year of prompt payment. If this is not clearly stated in the account information, call the bank and get clarification. You also need to pay close attention to the **annual interest rate on outstanding balances**, the **annual fee**, and **transaction charges on cash advances**. You should expect to pay more than the prevailing rates on unsecured cards, but the rates should not be oppressive.

The secured bank credit card starts helping your credit history right away. The bank will report your account history and payment information to the credit bureau after opening the account. After six months you will have a payment history on this account. At this point you could apply for an unsecured bank credit card or department store card and normally you will be accepted.

CARD OFFERS TO AVOID

Some "Credit Card" offers need to be avoided. These enticements are nothing more than come-ons that will do nothing to help your credit history. These are frequently seen on late-night television or in popular magazines. They promise a credit card with a limit of at least $2,000 with no credit check. The only catch is that there is a one-time processing fee of $75 or more. This processing fee goes to open the account and to prepare a catalog. The big catch is that the card can only be used to purchase goods from this catalog. The items are heavily marked up, and at least 25% of the purchase price must be put down in cash, along with extremely high charges for shipping, handling, and insurance.

The combination of the catalog fee and the other charges ensures that, even if the purchaser never makes a payment, the company makes a profit. These companies advertise that after a few months they will give you a letter attesting to your good credit that you can furnish to other creditors or the credit bureau. This type of one-shot reference is of very little utility, and these companies often will not assist you in getting the account listed with the credit bureau. They are not members of the credit association and do not report account holder histories to the credit bureaus.

In Chapter 9 we will go into other methods for getting account history information added to your credit report. However, for the person facing the problem of no credit history, the secured bank credit card is the fastest and easiest method to establish a credit history.

CHAPTER 6

CREDIT PROBLEM 2: NEGATIVE CREDIT INFORMATION

Negative credit information is anything on the credit report that will cause a potential creditor to deny extending credit. In this chapter two types of negative credit information are discussed. The first is delinquent account data. This is self-explanatory. The second is having excessive inquiry problems on the credit report. We will deal with these problems together because they involve using the same part of the Fair Credit Reporting Act.

DELINQUENT ACCOUNT DATA

Anyone can end up with delinquent payment data on his or her credit report. This happens in one of two ways. The first is when account information belonging to someone else gets on your credit report. The second is when, for one reason or another, you cannot pay your bills on time. Before we get into specifics, we need to look at *how much* negative information is fatal to a credit applicant.

One rule of thumb is that most creditors will overlook one delinquent account, even if it has degenerated into a total charge-off situation, if all the other accounts on the credit report are in order. The creditor will assume that this one exception was a legitimate disagreement between the creditor and the borrower. Creditors assume you are a creature of habit and you would not pay all of your other bills on time if you are a deadbeat.

ADDING A STATEMENT TO YOUR REPORT

The Fair Credit Reporting Act allows you to insert a short statement on the credit report stating your side of any dispute. If you have several account histories on your report and one is negative, this is the most expedient method to use. It also is the way to go if you only have one account on your credit report and it is negative. If this is your situation, after inserting the statement on the credit report, you should then apply for at least two secured bank credit card accounts. When the secured bank card issuer pulls your credit history, they will see the lone account along with your statement. Most secured card issuers will open an account in these circumstances.

After you obtain the secured credit cards, use them and make timely payments for at least a year. At the end of that period, apply for a regular unsecured bank card. The bank will pull the credit report and see the excellent payment history on the two secured accounts going back a year. They will assume the one account is a legitimate dispute.

The point is that you can insert the statement even if you were actually the one at fault. This method is applicable only when you have just *one* negative account on your credit report. Most people with serious credit problems have numerous negative accounts on their credit reports. The key is to remove enough negative credit history so that at most, only one delinquent account remains on the credit report. Ideally, you would like to have no delinquent accounts remaining on the credit report.

DISPUTING NEGATIVE ITEMS ON YOUR CREDIT REPORT

The first step to eliminating negative information is to obtain copies of your credit report from each of the three major credit bureaus. Once you have done this, label three folders with the name of each bureau. Staple the credit report to the inside front cover of each folder. On each credit report, circle the items that are negative. On a separate sheet of paper make a list of each negative item on each report. The next step is to begin the dispute procedure.

DISPUTE LETTER #1

Write a letter to each credit bureau, enclosing a copy of your credit report with the disputed items circled. Dispute a maximum of two items at a time. Some credit bureaus will provide a form on which to list disputes, which then accompanies their credit reports to consumers. If you receive one of these forms, use it. Make copies before you fill it out, so you can use the copies when you dispute other items in the future. Make copies of every letter you send. Sample letters of dispute appear in Appendix 6. Dispute Letter Number One initiates the dispute cycle. Mail the letter via Certified Mail, with a Return Receipt Requested. This gives you proof of the date the letter was mailed and proof that the credit bureau received the letter.

When the credit bureau receives the letter, it will begin the verification process. The credit bureau will pull a copy of your credit report to locate the items in question. They will then send a Request for Account Verification form to the creditors concerned. This is where the bureaucracy of the credit business comes into play. The Fair Credit Reporting Act says that the first time an account is not reverified within a reasonable period of time, it must be removed from the credit report. Even if the creditor later provides verification, the law does not allow this account to be put back on to the credit report. Some credit bureaus tried to do just this in prior years, but got into trouble for the practice.

DISPUTE LETTER #2

The Federal Trade Commission considers a reasonable time to be thirty days. If you have not heard anything from the credit bureau within three weeks after sending the first letter, send a second letter. This time, again request that these items be removed from your credit report, and tell the agency that the law requires them to do so. Say that if this is not done at once you will file a complaint with the Federal Trade Commission. Enclose a copy of your first letter. This letter is credit Dispute Letter Number Two, and a sample appears in Appendix 6.

This second letter should also be sent via Certified Mail, with Return Receipt Requested. Of course, a similar letter is sent to each bureau.

You might think that creditors would answer requests for account verification quickly. This is far from the case. Credit departments have a limited number of people working in them and they receive a lot of mail every day. Verifying data for the credit bureau is not their highest priority. Some creditors, however, will respond promptly to the credit bureau's request for account verification.

You can improve your chances of success with this method by disputing *older accounts*, and by disputing these accounts at certain times of the year. Let's assume that you were delinquent in paying a $200 account at a department store. The account was written off by the store two years ago. If you dispute this account, there is a very good chance that the creditor will no longer have any records concerning it. Thus that account cannot be verified.

It can also be smart to dispute accounts during the summer months when many people are on vacation, and any time between the middle of November and New Year's Day. In summer, many people in credit departments are on vacation. During the Thanksgiving through Christmas period creditors are attempting to open new accounts, so fewer staff are available to verify accounts for the credit bureau. These holidays also see a slowdown in verification because many credit staff are off work on the holidays.

DISPUTE LETTER #3

If you do not receive a response from the credit bureau two weeks after sending the second letter, a third letter should be sent. This will arrive at the credit bureau some six weeks after your first letter. The reasonable time provision of the Fair Credit Reporting Act will thus have elapsed. In this third letter, you should cite this fact and demand to have the items removed. You should also state that you will be filing a formal complaint with the Federal Trade Commission. Finally, you should state that, if you do not receive a copy of your credit report with the offending items removed within ten days, you will institute legal proceedings against the credit bureau.

Attach copies to this letter of the previous two letters you have set to the credit bureau. A sample third dispute letter is included in Appendix 6. This letter should also be sent via Certified Mail, with Return Receipt Requested. You have now fully documented your attempts to settle your dispute with the credit bureau. At this stage, you should file a complaint with the Federal Trade Commission. Let's now look at what the Federal Trade Commission will and will not do on behalf of a consumer.

FILING A COMPLAINT WITH THE FTC

Strictly speaking, The Federal Trade Commission is not interested in helping individual consumers solve a particular problem with the businesses it regulates. The FTC will get involved, however, when it receives a number of consumer complaints about a particular type of business. It then has the ability to force the offending establishment to conform with the Federal laws that regulate that particular business.

Credit bureaus received tens of thousands of complaints from consumers over their failure to investigate disputes promptly and to remove negative credit information in accordance with the law. A credit bureau complaint *will* be given attention by the FTC. Your letter to the FTC should include a brief description of your dispute with the credit bureau. The letter itself should be one page long and typewritten (see Appendix 6). Copies of your correspondence to the credit bureau, beginning with the first letter sent, should be attached.

The letter to the FTC should also be sent via Certified Mail, with Return Receipt Requested. It should be sent to the FTC office nearest your home. Here's the listing of all FTC offices. Write to the one nearest you.

FTC
11000 WILSHIRE BLVD
LOS ANGELES, CA 90024

FTC
901 MARKET ST, #570
SAN FRANCISCO, CA 94130

FTC
1405 CURTIS ST, #2900
DENVER, CO 80202

FEDERAL TRADE COMMISSION HEADQUARTERS
SIXTH AND PENNSYLVANIA AVENUE N.W.
WASHINGTON, DC 20580
(202) 326-2222

FTC
1718 PEACHTREE STREET N.W.
ATLANTA, GA 30367

FTC
55 EAST MONROE STREET, #1437
CHICAGO, IL 60603

FTC
10 CAUSEWAY STREET, #1184
BOSTON, MA 02222

FTC
150 WILLIAM STREET, #1300
NEW YORK, NY 10038

FTC
668 EUCLID AVENUE, #520-A
CLEVELAND, OH 44114

FTC
100 NORTH CENTRAL EXPRESSWAY
DALLAS, TX 75201

FTC
915 SECOND AVENUE
SEATTLE, WA 98174

After your letter arrives at the FTC office, it will be reviewed and decided if it warrants action. If it does, the FTC will institute its own action. The FTC can apply pressure on the credit bureau through a number of means. One of the most effective is to suggest changes in the law to force the credit bureaus to become more consumer friendly. This has already occurred, and it is one reason that credit bureaus are instituting policies that are more beneficial to consumers. FTC action is also why a number of bills are before Congress to tighten the regulations governing credit bureaus. Quite often a letter from the FTC is enough to get the credit bureau to relent and to delete the items in question.

At this point you have fully documented your case against the credit bureau. You have created a paper trail that can act as evidence in any future legal proceeding against the credit bureau. However, before you institute legal proceedings, as a last resort, you should go through this dispute cycle two items at a time on each credit report from each of the major bureaus.

After you have gone through this cycle, the next step is to take stock of what you have and have not accomplished. You will probably have some combination of the following results:

1.   SOME CREDIT BUREAUS WILL NOT HAVE RESPONDED AT ALL
2.   SOME ITEMS WERE REMOVED TO YOUR SATISFACTION
3.   SOME CREDITORS RECONFIRMED THE DISPUTED ITEMS

Before discussing specific strategies for legal action, we need to look at removal of excessive inquiry information from the credit report.

EXCESSIVE INQUIRIES

Technically, the Fair Credit Reporting Act does not give consumers the same rights to dispute inquiries as it does for them to dispute account information. However, the FTC has taken a broad interpretation of the law in this regard, and applies it to inquiries as well.

If you have made the mistake of applying for credit over and over with one rejection after another, the excessive inquiry problem will apply to you. Inquiries on your credit report should always be challenged on the basis that they were not authorized by you. Remember, a credit report cannot be obtained legally unless you have given your consent. If your credit report lists six inquiries, challenge four of them as being unauthorized. Challenge the four oldest ones.

Inquiries are easier to remove from a credit report than account information because the creditor has little or no interest in verifying them. A creditor that has lost money on an account with you has an interest in keeping your credit record blackened. This is the creditor's "revenge" for having lost money with your account. A simple inquiry is another matter completely. Many creditors who will verify account information to the credit bureau will not bother to verify a dispute over an unauthorized inquiry. In fact, if the inquiry was made a couple of months earlier, the creditor may no longer even have records of your credit application. Dispute the inquiries after you have gone through the full dispute cycle on the account items you want removed.

TAKING LEGAL ACTION

Legal proceedings against a credit bureau can be instituted through three routes of action. The Fair Credit Reporting Act explicitly states that the Federal law does not invalidate state and local laws that apply to credit bureaus. The credit bureaus wish that this were not the case since some states have very aggressive laws regulating the credit bureau industry. Thus the options are: (1) a consumer can bring a suit against a credit bureau in Federal Court under the provisions of the Federal law; (2) the credit bureau can be sued in State Court under the applicable state law; or (3) you can sue the credit bureau in Small Claims Court for damages. The Small Claims Court cannot force the credit bureau to change your credit file, but it can award you monetary damages against the bureau.

Initiating legal proceedings against the credit bureau is the least desirable course of action because of the time and expense involved. Before you begin legal proceedings against the credit bureau, there are other avenues you can pursue that may achieve the desired result faster. The first thing is to remember that you can dispute an item more than once. After you have gone through the dispute cycle once on every item you want removed, take the following steps:

1. IF YOUR STATE HAS A LAW REGULATING CREDIT BUREAUS, FILE A COMPLAINT WITH THE STATE CONSUMER AFFAIRS AGENCY THAT REGULATES THE CREDIT BUREAUS.

2. INITIATE THE DISPUTE CYCLE A SECOND TIME ON UNREMOVED ITEMS.

You can find out if your state has a law regulating credit bureaus by contacting your local district attorney's office. They will likely have brochures that explain your rights under the law. State laws are often more effective because the credit bureau will have accessed a local affiliate near your home for your credit report. Many times this affiliate is an independent business that cannot afford static from state regulators.

State regulators also can put pressure on the national bureau by threatening to prevent it from doing business in its territory unless the bureau conforms to the state law. If you file a complaint with the state agency regulating credit bureaus, and they see from your documentation you have already attempted to resolve the matter under the Federal law, they may take action at once. State agencies often are more responsive than are Federal agencies.

Going through the dispute cycle a second time may result in the removal of more negative items. Follow exactly the same procedure as the first time. If, after the second cycle, you are still left with creditors who insist on responding to the credit bureau's request for account verification, you need to take the matter up with the creditor directly.

DEALING DIRECTLY WITH CREDITORS

Credit bureaus have tried to convince creditors that their interests are 100% congruent. The bureaus send subscribing creditors information all the time about how important it is that they respond to bureau requests for account verification in order to protect the integrity of credit files. The bureaus also strenuously ask creditors not to strike deals with delinquent borrowers. These deals usually are an agreement that the creditor will no longer report the account on the credit history in exchange for a payment agreement.

There are two types of delinquent accounts. A creditor will carry a delinquent account on its books for only so long. When an account is 30 days late, the credit department's regular staff will make a telephone call and/or send a letter to the borrower with a gentle reminder to send a check. If the account is one of long standing with a good payment history, no direct contact is likely to be made with the borrower. The creditor assumes that the delinquency at this point is just an oversight.

After 60 days of nonpayment, the account will be turned over to the creditor's in-house collection department. At this point, the creditor has by no means given up on the account. The collection department will make an effort to have the borrower become current again on the account. This is especially true if the account was previously paid on time over an extended period. The collection staff will try to determine if the customer has fallen on hard times. If so, they will attempt to work out a modified payment arrangement until the customer's financial situation improves.

When an account is 120 days or more delinquent, the creditor is no longer interested in maintaining a future relationship with the borrower. At this point the creditor's only concern is to minimize losses on the account. The in-house collection staff will send a series of demanding letters to the borrower, and will begin making a series of telephone calls. The calls and letters will threaten to damage the borrower's credit history and will hint at legal action to collect the debt. The in-house collection staff seeks to frighten the debtor into paying so that the account will not need to be written off.

If no payment has been received after 120 days, the creditor will write off the value of the account and refer it to an outside collection agency. This is the last alternative the creditor wants to be forced into taking. When an account has to be written off, it becomes a loss on the creditor's books, and if the outside collection agency later collects money on the account, that agency typically keeps 50% of the amount they recoup.

This information gives you strong leverage when dealing with a creditor that continues to reverify an account referred for collection. The first step you should take in this situation is to deal with the *creditor*, not the collection agency. Call the creditor's in-house department and tell them you would like to work out a payment arrangement. Collection department personnel are rated on how much they are able to recover on bad accounts. The possibility that a settlement could be made on an account that has already been written off will certainly interest a manager in the collection department.

The agreement you will want to reach involves you paying about **60% of the total dollar value of the account**, either in a lump sum or in a few installments. In return for this you want the account no longer reported to credit bureaus by the outside collection agency, and if the account still shows up on the credit report by the original creditor, you want this entry removed as well. The account must *disappear* from your credit report. Do not accept an offer to have the account marked "Paid in Full" on the credit report. This does you no good, because the fact that you had an account referred for collection is still on your credit report. Most creditors have no interest in doing business with people who have collection accounts on their credit reports.

This agreement between you and the creditor should be made in *writing*. Do not send any money to the creditor until you receive a written agreement, signed by a manager authorized to strike such a deal. A sample letter for such a payoff deal is given in Appendix 6.

If you have gone through a second dispute cycle, and have attempted to reach payoff arrangements with your creditors, but are still left with multiple negative credit entries on your credit report, it is time to consider **legal action**. You can accomplish two goals through legal action. The first is to obtain damages from the credit bureau and/or its local affiliate. This can be accomplished most efficiently via the Small Claims Court.

Many states now allow Small Claims courts to hear disputes up to a value of $5,000. The Small Claims court judge will want to see that you have attempted to resolve the dispute with the credit bureau on your own. This is where your paper trail of letters becomes so important. In some states the Small Claims Court will allow you to base your claim on the Federal law, others will require you to base it on the relevant state law.

To strengthen your case for Small Claims or State court, it is best to initiate your disputes directly with the local affiliate of the major bureaus, as opposed to requesting your report from the corporate consumer addresses of the major bureau. This also makes it easier to identify who you will be suing. Small Claims Court procedures are simple, and you need to contact your Small Claims Court clerk for information and the necessary forms for filing a dispute. Remember that the Small Claims Court cannot force the credit bureau to change the information in their files. The court can only force the credit bureau to pay you damages for having suffered from the adverse information in their files.

The second method of legal redress is to file a lawsuit in State Court under your state credit reporting law. This requires a lawyer. Civil lawsuits often take years to be heard and work their way through the appeal process. One way to expedite this procedure is to ask the court for what is known as "**Injunctive Relief**" against the credit bureau until your case is heard. Essentially, under injunctive relief, the judge orders the credit bureau to stop reporting the disputed credit information until the case can be heard. Your attorney can make this motion on the basis that this disputed information is causing you harm — credit denial, employment denial, etc. — and this injunction will allow you to function until the case is tried.

The same tactic can be used under the Federal law. You must consult an attorney. Many lawyers now give a free initial consultation, or charge a small amount for a first meeting. Make sure to bring all of your documentation to this meeting. Some attorneys may even take your case on a no fee contingency basis, where they are paid a percentage of what is collected against the credit bureau.

The methods described in this chapter are applicable if you have at least one account on your credit history that has a good payment history. If you have no good accounts on your credit history, and have gone through the dispute cycle twice, but you still have negative information left on your credit report, it is advisable to seek another method of credit repair that gives you a clean, but empty, credit report much faster. For some people this is the only alternative. Before we discuss this method of credit repair, we need to look at negative credit data caused by public record information and credit bureau warning programs.

CHAPTER 7

CREDIT PROBLEM 3: NEGATIVE PUBLIC RECORD DATA

Pubic record information is subject to many errors when it is reported on credit histories. One well-known example illustrates this problem very well.

One of the major bureaus contracted with an outside vendor to obtain local property tax records in New England. This vendor sent individuals from county to county to check records for people who had not paid property taxes and thus had liens filed against their homes. This information was written down from the applicable records at the courthouse or town hall. The credit bureau then matched these names and addresses against its files. A tax lien was duly recorded on each applicable credit report.

In one small town the property tax record listing was not a listing of people who had not paid their taxes, *but of those who had*. Soon afterward, almost the entire adult population of that town started to experience credit problems. People who wanted to refinance their mortgages were told that they were in default because they had failed to pay their property taxes. Creditors who pulled routine credit reports on the residents' existing accounts threatened to cancel existing lines of credit unless people paid their taxes at once.

The ensuing publicity and threat of legal action by the townsfolk ensured rapid action on the part of the credit bureau to correct its records. This incident is typical of the problem of negative and/or inaccurate public record information appearing on credit reports. Fortunately, there are ways to deal with this.

Public record information is disputed on credit reports in the same way as credit history information. The only difference is that the credit bureau will send an entry verification letter to the clerk of the court concerned. The most common public record problem for consumers is a **bankruptcy filing**. Most creditors consider consumer bankruptcy laws nothing more than legalized stealing. Credit bureaus can report bankruptcy information on a credit report for ten years. There are two ways that bankruptcy information can successfully be disputed and removed from the credit report.

A bankruptcy filing will be matched against the credit report files by name, Social Security Number, and sometimes birthdate and address. The easiest way to dispute a bankruptcy record is to wait until the file has been sent from the courthouse to the nearest Federal Archive center. When a request comes to that center from the credit bureau, the bankruptcy must be verified by actually seeing the file. A computer extract is not legal verification of the event.

If you went through bankruptcy proceedings three or more years ago, there is a good chance that your file is no longer at the courthouse where the bankruptcy relief occurred. The time that elapses before a file is sent to the Federal Archive varies from court to court. Call the bankruptcy court where your proceedings took place to determine if the file is still at the courthouse. If it is, go to the bankruptcy court in question and fill out a request for your bankruptcy records to be sent to the courthouse for you to review.

The next day send a letter to the credit bureau disputing the bankruptcy on your credit report. The credit bureau will send a letter to the bankruptcy court clerk asking for confirmation of the bankruptcy. The clerk will send for the records from the Archive, but they will already be in transit because of *your* request. The clerk will not make a connection between the two requests, since many requests are received every day for records.

A week to ten days later, you should receive a form letter from the bankruptcy court clerk informing you that your records are available in a public viewing section at the courthouse. The letter will also state that if you do not view the records by a certain date, usually within two to three weeks, they will be returned to the Federal Archive.

The Archive will not be able to locate your bankruptcy records to comply with the request from the credit bureau. The clerk will thus send a form to the credit bureau stating that the record could not be located. A similar strategy may be used for any public record that has been sent to an archive after a period of time.

Another strategy that can be used when disputing public record information is to increase the time it takes for the credit bureau to verify an entry. One way to do this is to lodge your dispute with a distant branch of the bureau. If you live in Oregon, you could file your dispute with a branch of the credit bureau, say, in Florida. When you mail your dispute letter, you *must not use* a return address from a commercial mail receiving service. Use the address of a secretarial service. Commercial mail receiving services trigger credit bureau warning programs. We will examine these again in the next chapter.

A dispute utilizing a distant credit bureau branch proceeds just like any other dispute. This is most effective with public record information such as tax liens, local county court judgments, and also bankruptcies. A combination of the remoteness of the credit bureau branch, along with the fact that court clerks are overworked, may conspire to have your negative public record data removed.

CHAPTER 8

CREDIT PROBLEM 4: CREDIT BUREAU WARNING PROGRAMS

Credit bureaus themselves cause many problems for consumers by their warning programs. These programs are designed to help creditors identify people who may become bad credit risks or people attempting to jettison a bad credit history. These "enhancements" to the basic credit report generally cost the subscriber a little extra for each report ordered. Some of these features are included with the base price of the credit report. The problem with these programs is that you can be wrongly labeled as a bad risk.

Warning programs operate by comparing information already stored in the credit bureau database with the information supplied by the credit applicant. Certain differences between the two will cause a warning to be broadcast across the face of the credit report. The credit bureaus have so many of these warning programs that *most credit reports now contain at least one such warning.*

MAIL FORWARDING AND TELEPHONE ANSWERING SERVICES

In the previous chapter, I mentioned that you should not use a mail forwarding service when dealing with a credit bureau. The use of such a service triggers a warning program at the credit bureaus. Credit bureaus maintain files that list all mail forwarding agencies and check cashing establishments that rent mailboxes to their clients. This information is gathered nationwide from telephone directories and is entered into a central file. Telephone numbers associated with these establishments are also put in the database.

If a consumer applies for credit using one of these agencies as his home address, a warning will flash across the credit report that the address being used is that of a mail forwarding service. Most creditors will turn down the application right then and there. The credit bureaus say that this database helps protect credit grantors from fraud and uncollectable accounts, but it also penalizes anyone who uses one of these services.

Many consumers receive mail at such places for security or privacy. Some consumers receive mail at such commercial locations because they receive packages often and do not want to have to go to the post office at inconvenient times to pick them up. The point is that the credit bureau could care less that they injure the credit of many good people to blacken the credit of a few.

Similar credit bureau warning programs apply to telephone answering services. If the address or telephone number of a telephone answering service is given on a credit application, a warning will flash across the credit report. The warning will identify the name and address of the answering service used.

NAME VARIATIONS

Perhaps the worst of the credit bureau warning programs deals with the credit applicant's name. Any difference in the spelling of the applicant's name (often just a simple input error by the clerk entering the application data into the computer) can trigger these programs. A one-letter variation in the spelling of your name caused by a clerical mistake can label your credit report as a loss risk.

SOCIAL SECURITY NUMBERS

Another warning program deals with Social Security Numbers. Credit report retrieval process involves using part of the Social Security Number (SSN). People who are attempting to shed a poor credit history often change a digit or two of their SSN. The Social Security Warning programs attempt to prevent applicants from doing this.

There are three SSN warning programs. The first compares the SSN furnished on the application form with the one already in the database for the individual concerned. If there is a difference, a warning will be flashed on the screen along with the previous SSN in the file. This program is most often triggered by an applicant accidentally transposing a digit on the application form or by clerical error. The credit bureau computer makes no differentiation between this type of honest error and a deliberate attempt to alter the SSN.

The second SSN warning program attempts to determine whether more than one person is using the same number. This program assumes that the first person in the file who uses a given SSN is the person to whom the number has legitimately been assigned. This programmed assumption can cause numerous problems for honest individuals. Consider the following example...

Assume that an individual applies for credit and accidentally transposes two digits in his Social Security Number. On his credit report a warning is flashed that the number given differs from the one already in the file for this person. This occurs so frequently that some creditors will overlook this warning on the credit report of someone with established credit. A year later, a different, first-time, applicant requests credit giving her true Social Security Number, which happens to be the same as the transposed SSN on the first person's application. The credit bureau's program will be activated even though the SSN legitimately belongs to the female applicant. The male applicant mistakenly used this number first, and thus the credit bureau computer wrongly assumes the female applicant is attempting to jettison a bad credit history.

The last SSN warning program is designed to identify impossible numbers, or numbers that are possible, but that have not yet been issued.

DISPUTING WARNING PROGRAM DATA

How can these warning programs be disputed? Just like any other item. In the case of Social Security Numbers, you might enclose a photocopy of your SSN card with the dispute letter. It is not as easy to remove address warning programs. The credit bureaus claim that creditors have a legitimate interest in knowing the physical address of applicants. The best way to remove address warnings is simply to use a real street address. Ask a friend or relative if you can use their address for credit applications.

Some people have such severe credit problems that even the methods discussed in the last few chapters are of limited utility. These people may have creditors who absolutely refuse to negotiate a payoff arrangement of a debt, or creditors who always verify account information when a dispute letter arrives from the credit bureau. If all of the previous methods have left you with more than one bad account on your credit report, or you desire to enter the world of credit quickly, this last method is for you. It is called *file segregation*. It is the only method that will remove all of your negative credit history quickly and inexpensively, and is detailed in the next chapter.

CHAPTER 9

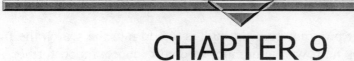

FILE SEGREGATION

File segregation exploits the way that the computers at a credit bureau attempt to create files on individuals who do not yet have an existing credit history. It also makes use of the fact that, despite the millions of people who are listed in credit bureau files, only a limited number of surnames account for the vast majority of the files. File segregation also takes advantage of the fact that the credit bureaus' great zeal to collect negative information on people has caused many individuals to have more than one file at a given credit bureau.

The file segregation technique allows you to re-enter the credit system with a totally blank slate. You can jettison all of your negative credit information. This includes a negative account history, excessive inquiries, credit bureau warning programs, and negative public record information. To understand how file segregation works, we must examine how the credit bureau's computer locates one particular file from the millions that it stores.

The computers at the credit bureau are designed to create a new credit file only when no file already exists. *This is the key to the file segregation technique.* By altering enough of the identifying information on the credit report, the applicant can cause the credit bureau computer to respond with the statement: "No record found." When this magical statement is made, the credit bureau computer creates a new credit file with the new information. This blank credit file can now be retrieved by furnishing the same personal information in the future. The file will contain no negative credit history or public record information. The only items in this credit file will be the identifying information and the name of the creditor making the inquiry in the inquiry section. Once the blank credit file is created, it is a simple matter to add positive credit history information by one of the methods discussed previously.

Credit bureau computers retrieve individual credit files by going through a gradual winnowing process that progressively uses more and more bits of the personal identifiers from the application. When only one credit report is identified, the computer will stop searching and print out the report located. Essentially, the personal identifying information is reduced to a string of computer code that locates one individual's file.

The initial information with which the computer works is the **first ten letters of the applicant's last name**. The computer will search for all files having the same first ten letters in the last name. If there is only one credit history at this point, it will be pulled by the computer. However, the odds are that there are tens of thousands of credit reports with the same first ten letters of the last name.

The next step the computer program goes through is to add into the search the **first three letters of the first name**. This narrows the number of credit reports much further. Then the **middle initial** will be added. If there are still numerous credit reports with the same name information, the **first initial of the applicant's spouse** will be added. At this point, there are probably still hundreds of credit reports that correspond to this information. In the case of a very common name, there could still be tens of thousands of credit reports retrievable.

The **first five digits of the street number** will now be added, along with the **first five letters of the street name**. The chances are that only a few reports now will be identified. The final information used by the credit bureau computer program is the **Zip code**, **previous address**, and **Social Security Number**. When these identifiers are added, only one credit report will be found — or none. One credit bureau bases its entire retrieval system on the Social Security Number, but this has resulted in many problems. A wrongly typed SSN will not only cause the problems mentioned in the previous chapter, but will create a new file as well, with all of the warnings on it.

You might wonder why the credit bureaus don't utilize a file retrieval system based only on the full name, date of birth, and Social Security Number. The answer is the sheer number of records that must be maintained. The major bureaus typically maintain files on over 100 million people. Many of these people have identical names and birthdates, and their Social Security Numbers might be close enough to cause major problems when using such data as retrieval information.

HOW FILE SEGREGATION WORKS

The file segregation technique changes enough information so that no existing credit record can be found and a new, untarnished one will be created.

CHANGING YOUR NAME

The first step involves altering your name enough so that, to the computer, you are a different person. The simplest and most effective technique is to transpose your first and middle names. So, if your credit history lists you presently as Diana Kate Jones, your new credit identity will be Kate Diana Jones.

ALTERING YOUR ADDRESS

The next step involves altering your current address, as well as your previous address. These addresses cannot be any address at which you have lived in the past or present. You must exercise some caution when picking this address. As mentioned previously, it cannot be that of a commercial mail receiving service or check cashing office that rents mailboxes. Instead, see if a friend will allow you to use his or her address, or arrange to rent an address from a secretarial or office rental service. These agencies can be found in the telephone directory, and often will have a package deal that will allow you to use their address and telephone number for one monthly fee.

ALTERING YOUR SOCIAL SECURITY NUMBER

The next identifier that must be altered is your Social Security Number. *You cannot continue to use the same SSN.* The credit bureau warning programs will quickly identify this number and show your unaltered name on the credit report. This will tell a prospective creditor that you are attempting to create a new credit file. There are three ways of altering your SSN.

The best method is to simply apply for another Social Security Number. There is no law that prohibits an individual from having more than one number. The Social Security Administration will ask you why you want another number. This can be explained by simply stating that someone else has been illegally using your Social Security Number. After providing required identification, you should receive your new number about two weeks after you apply for it. Another method is to make up a new Social Security Number. The problem with this method is that you may accidentally create a number that is already being used by someone in the credit files. This will trigger the bureau's warning programs.

The final method is to use the Social Security Number of a friend or relative who has no credit and will never be in the credit bureau files. They would have to be willing to give their consent. *This method is not recommended.* Apply for a new Social Security Number.

There is also a method advertised by credit repair clinics that should be avoided. It involves applying for what is known as an Employer Identification Number from the Internal Revenue Service. The credit repair clinics advise using this number in place of the Social Security Number. This method is not very effective because the Employer Identification Number will not always correspond to a valid Social Security Number Grouping. The credit bureaus have become wise to this method and are now programming their computers to detect this ploy.

NOW GET A NEW CREDIT FILE

Once you have a new SSN, address, phone number, etc., write out the following information.

MODIFIED NAME

NEW SOCIAL SECURITY NUMBER

NEW HOME ADDRESS

NEW FORMER ADDRESS

BIRTHDATE

NEW HOME TELEPHONE NUMBER

The birthdate need not be changed. I recommend obtaining a new telephone number to complete the break with your old credit past. This new information needs to be written on a sheet of paper so that this credit file will be retrieved every time you apply for credit using your new file. A sample File Segregation worksheet is on the next page.

Pick up a credit card application from any bank. It really does not matter where the application is from. The application will be declined due to no existing credit history. The process of the credit application being denied will cause a new credit file to be established. When you receive the rejection letter, take it to your local credit bureau and obtain a free copy of your report. This will be proof of your new clean credit file. You can then proceed to build positive credit through a secured credit card.

CREDIT TERMS

Dealing with credit bureaus is only half of the secret to taking control of your credit future. The other side of the coin involves understanding how creditors size you up and determine not only if you will be extended credit, but on what terms. Millions of people are able to obtain credit only on very unfavorable terms because creditors consider them less desirable than other applicants. In the next chapter we will see what these secret criteria are and how you can become one of the people to whom creditors extend the best terms.

FILE SEGREGATION WORKSHEET

FULL NAME: _____
BIRTHDATE: _____
SOCIAL SECURITY NUMBER: _____
CURRENT ADDRESS: _____
CITY/STATE/ZIP: _____
PREVIOUS ADDRESS: _____
CITY/STATE/ZIP: _____
HOME TELEPHONE NUMBER: _____

ALTERATION INSTRUCTIONS:

1) Use middle name as first name, use first name as middle name.
2) Use new SS Number as described in text
3) Obtain new address to replace current address
4) Previous address can be any street address at which you have never lived or used when applying for credit.
5) Obtain new telephone number.
6) Other data can remain the same.

NEW NAME: _____
NEW SOCIAL SECURITY NUMBER: _____
NEW ADDRESS: _____
NEW CITY/STATE/ZIP: _____
NEW PREVIOUS ADDRESS: _____
NEW PREVIOUS CITY/STATE/ZIP: _____
NEW HOME TELEPHONE: _____

After you have determined the new information, write it down and save it. This information must be used every time you apply for credit to recall the new credit file.

CHAPTER 10

INSIDER CREDITOR SECRETS: PART ONE

The concept of **credit culture** is always uppermost in the minds of creditors. We have seen that the credit industry is unique in the fact that no other business solicits clients with the expectation of *rejecting* many of those who wish to patronize their services. This is called credit culture and can be summed up by the old saying "Many are called but few are chosen." Millions of people with blank credit files find that they are always part of the many. Even people who were once part of the few can become part of the many due to no fault of their own. The vital point is that you can become one of the many even with a good credit history.

Consider the difference in credit practices of a local finance company and a typical Travel and Entertainment card company. The finance company charges a very high interest rate and has very flexible lending practices. Typical finance company loans involve small monthly payments over very long periods of time. This allows them to lend very profitably to low wage individuals and to collect large amounts of interest income over the years. In sort, the finance company specializes in lending to people who really need the money badly.

A Travel and Entertainment card company has a totally different focus. It markets itself to people who do not really *need* another credit card. Its focus is to give busy people an additional facility when traveling. They want you to use their card for a cash advance when traveling, not because you need the money, but due to the convenience value. Just go to an automated teller machine and get cash quickly. Of course, a small fee will be charged for this service.

These examples present diametrically opposed credit cultures. The problem for many individuals is that they are seen by creditors as poor risks and do not meet any lender's credit culture. One part of this problem concerns employment. Millions of people work in jobs that creditors consider unstable, even if the individual has held the same job for years. People who hold these jobs are automatically rejected for credit by creditor scoring and screening systems. The fair credit laws do not prevent this practice as long as creditors discriminate equally against people holding such "undesirable" employment.

The following list is a typical (but not necessarily complete) roster of employment that is usually considered unacceptable to a creditor:

WAITRESSES AND WAITERS

OTHER RESTAURANT WORKERS UNLESS MANAGER

GROCERY STORE WORKERS BELOW MANAGER

CONVENIENCE STORE WORKERS

HOTEL AND MOTEL WORKERS BELOW MANAGER

MOVIE PROJECTIONISTS

HAIR STYLISTS

SELF-EMPLOYED PEOPLE

UNSKILLED OR SEMISKILLED LABORERS

ACTORS, UNLESS WELL KNOWN

As you can see, this list encompasses millions of workers. When these people are able to obtain credit, it is often on very bad terms. In many ways, creditors have not changed with the times. This is especially true for people who are self-employed. Most creditors view self-employed people as unemployed. The only exception is if it is a well-known and long-established company or firm. This is a hypocritical perspective to have in the late 1990s.

Many people who became unemployed during the recession have started new businesses with money from severance agreements or corporate buyouts. Most creditors view these people as poor risks.

The solution to this problem involves using a little inventiveness. Each situation is a little different, but some general guidelines can be given. We need to return again to what is and is not verified on a credit application. The first situation is that of a person who has established credit, but now finds himself or herself unemployed. Perhaps this person needs some additional credit to bridge the gap until new employment is found.

In this situation, the person could continue to **list the former employer** on the credit application. If the individual has an established credit history, a potential creditor will accept the credit report as sufficient verification of the application information. If you know you will be laid off in the near future, it would be smart to apply for credit now, before the layoff occurs. As long as you are not committing credit fraud, this will cause few problems.

People who are stuck in jobs that creditors do not like can improve their situations by **describing their employment in different terms**. A low-level computer programmer could describe himself as a computer scientist. A restaurant hostess could describe herself as a "Customer Service Manager." Often, a talk with your boss about your need to establish credit will get his or her agreement to go along. You can **inflate your salary** by a few hundred dollars a month without worry because this information is almost never verified by creditors. Most companies will not release salary details of employees over the telephone.

Some people have jobs rated unfavorably by creditors and it is not possible to describe them in a better fashion. Stronger methods must be used in this situation. A **suitable employment reference** can be created to win the creditor's favor.

To set up an employment reference find a secretarial or office service that offers a low cost "corporate identity" package. Once you have done this come up with a company name, being careful not to choose a name of a corporation already in existence. After this has been done, obtain a telephone number for the company. This can be obtained three ways at minimal cost. The first is to get a listing in the company name from the local telephone company. If this is too expensive, find out if the office/secretarial service offers telephone answering at a reduced price with the office identity package. The only drawback with this is that the number will not be listed with directory assistance.

The best alternative is to arrange a business telephone number with a voice mail company. These companies allow you to rent one of their numbers as your own. You record a message for callers to hear when they call. The voice mail company can arrange to get the telephone number listed in the directory under the company name. The voice mail telephone number can also be set up if you don't have a home telephone. This will give you a listed home telephone number when you apply for secured credit card accounts. Depending on how far you want to go, you could even incorporate the company in the State of Delaware for under $100 by mail. Then the company is a legal entity. The final step would be to get company letterhead printed up at a local quick printer.

Once you have created the company, you can give yourself any job title you wish. Use some common sense. Pick a position that creditors look on with favor, but don't overreach. Most executive vice presidents already have established credit histories. Pick a salary within range for the position claimed.

Just as creditors have occupations they dislike, they also have occupations they view with high regard. A partial listing of these occupations includes the following:

PROFESSIONAL DEGREED ENGINEERS AND SCIENTISTS

MEDICAL DOCTORS

REGISTERED NURSES

OPTOMETRISTS AND PSYCHOLOGISTS

SKILLED PROFESSIONAL TECHNICIANS

UNIVERSITY AND COLLEGE PROFESSORS

FEDERAL AND STATE GOVERNMENT EMPLOYEES

PROFESSIONAL PILOTS WITH MAJOR AIRLINES

UNIONIZED WORKERS AT MAJOR COMPANIES

PROFESSIONAL CORPORATE MANAGERS

ATTORNEYS

ACCOUNTANTS WITH DEGREES (NOT BOOKKEEPERS)

The general idea is clear. Creditors prefer these types of people. They believe that individuals in these occupations have above average job stability, and in the normal course of time, will have increased earnings year to year. By manipulating your job title, you can ensure that you are one of those on whom credit grantors smile.

The credit system is remarkably disorganized. In the next chapter, we will reveal ways that you can get unsolicited offers for preapproved credit cards and also show how an individual can obtain as much unsecured credit as possible.

YOU'RE PREAPPROVED!

CHAPTER 11

INSIDER CREDITOR SECRETS: PART TWO

Some people are lucky enough to receive preapproved credit card solicitations in the mail. All the recipient must do is sign the short form indicating they want the card offered, and about two weeks later it will be in their mailbox. People without credit who badly need it often find this unbelievable. The good news for the credit poor is that there are specific steps they can take to greatly increase their chances of getting a preapproved offer of a credit card.

First, let's define more precisely what is meant by a preapproved offer of credit. The Federal Government issued some rules that creditors must follow when making these offers.

Creditors abused preapproved offers in the past by sending out solicitations that would say they were preapproved when in reality they were not.

OBTAINING PREAPPROVED CREDIT CARDS

Preapproved credit card offers are essentially junk mail. Creditors found that if they did a targeted mailing of a regular solicitation for a credit card, there would be almost no response from the public. Creditors then began making mass mailings with the word "Preapproved" on them, and the response rate went up immensely. The fine print elsewhere on the solicitation would state "Preapproved Subject To Credit Qualification." The consumer did not see this fine print. After many complaints about this practice, the Federal government changed the rules. *The new rules say that anyone offered a preapproved credit card offer by mail, must receive the credit offered if the request form is returned to the creditor.* The request form can be used only to confirm the identity of the borrower. This is why preapproved card offers typically ask for your Social Security Number and telephone number on the response card.

Prospects for preapproved credit card solicitations are compiled from two sources. One is from the credit bureau itself through a process called **prescreening**. A creditor will contact a credit bureau and request a list of, say, 20,000 people who meet certain financial criteria. These criteria involve items such as income, type of employment, approximate average value of a home in the neighborhood, and types of credit cards already held. By scanning its files, the credit bureau can create a list of people who will meet the creditor's requirements. The creditor pays a fee for each name, and that fee is much less than for pulling a full credit history on each person.

The second way creditors obtain names and addresses of preapproved customers is from **mailing lists**, particularly from magazines and specialized professional journals. Magazines send detailed questionnaires to their subscribers to create a profile of a typical reader. These questionnaires will ask about income, type of employment, home ownership, number of vehicles, educational attainment, and many other personal facts. This profile then allows the magazine to market itself to advertisers more effectively and to charge higher advertising rates.

Magazines also make money from selling their subscriber lists to other businesses, and creditors are major purchasers of these lists. Specialized technical journals have even better demographics for creditors wanting to send out preapproved mass mailings. It is obvious that most of the subscribers to, say, *The New England Journal of Medicine*, are physicians. A preapproved credit offer to the subscribers of this publication will go to high income, good credit individuals who are hard to reach by other methods. Purchasing a magazine subscriber list is cheaper than purchasing similar data from the credit bureau.

What magazines should you subscribe to in order to increase your chances of receiving a preapproved credit offer? Pick specialized magazines for medical or technical professionals. You need not be a doctor or scientist to subscribe to these journals. Popular newsstand magazines include the following:

BUSINESS WEEK

FORBES

FORTUNE

SCIENTIFIC AMERICAN

THE ECONOMIST

THE WALL STREET JOURNAL

Carefully read any preapproved credit card offer you receive. Be on the lookout for words that are similar to preapproved offers, but in reality are not. The words "Preselected," "Prescreened," or "Prechosen" are *not* preapproved credit offers. Some creditors attempt to use this language to get around the law and to increase response rates.

SPECIAL QUALIFICATION CARDS

There are other ways to break into the credit system. Another credit industry "Back Door" is special qualification credit cards. A good example can be found on any college campus. College students can obtain all major bankcards, and even an American Express card, without a previous credit history. A short application must be completed along with proof of student status. Approval is almost automatic, as long as the student has no bad credit. The limits on these cards are low, usually no more than a thousand dollars. The following banks are among those that issue credit cards to students under special criteria.

CITIBANK

SIGNET BANK

BANK OF BALTIMORE

BANK OF WICHITA

MBNA BANK

WELLS FARGO BANK

BANK OF AMERICA

DISCOVER CARD

CHASE MANHATTAN BANK

ATT UNIVERSAL CARD

AMERICAN EXPRESS

You can become eligible for one of these cards by registering for one class at a local college. These student offers can be an excellent way to break into the credit system. The banks recruit the student market because they know that in the future these students will be among the top income earners in the country. So they waive income and credit requirements to tap into this lucrative market. They also know that, if for some reason Junior cannot make his minimum payment on time, mom and dad usually will.

A few years ago there was a man who regularly appeared on late-night television with an hour-long commercial that purported to tell people how they could accumulate up to a million dollars in unsecured credit on credit cards. He billed himself as a credit card millionaire. His program recommended this student-application method for obtaining large amounts of unsecured credit to subsequently be used for investment purposes. Automobiles and property could also be purchased free and clear with no liens or mortgages held by banks. In theory, it is possible to execute a variant of this strategy, but there are some real risks involved.

ACCUMULATING UNSECURED CREDIT LINES

The first step in accumulating large amounts of unsecured available credit lines is to target which creditors you approach. This assumes that you have built your initial credit rating via a secured credit card account. When you first set out to build your credit, you want to select banks that have easier credit standards and that are seeking new business. These banks are where you will target your applications.

Credit card issuers that **charge higher interest rates** will be more lax in approving new accounts. These banks will also tend to grant higher credit limits on new accounts. They normally operate in states that impose no interest rate limits on out-of-state customers. South Dakota and Delaware are two such states. Credit card issuers that issue very low rate interest cards minimize their credit exposure by having very low credit limits and/or higher credit qualification criteria. These card issuers often decline a credit applicant who already has three or four other cards or does not have a very long and extensive credit history.

The goal is to have each credit application approved, and to improve your financial profile with each subsequent application for credit. This is done by **manipulating the employment information** on the application. As we have seen, salary details and job titles are not verified by most creditors. By increasing your salary and improving your job title, subsequent creditors will want to give you higher limits.

This second part of this strategy involves **removing the inquiries from your credit report** from time to time. More than three or four credit inquiries on a credit report in the last six months can trigger credit bureau warning programs. As you follow this strategy of building credit, you must periodically remove these inquiries. This is done by disputing the inquiries at six-month intervals. Each inquiry should be disputed, one or two at a time, the oldest ones first. Once these are removed you can start applying for more credit.

DRAWBACKS TO USING UNSECURED CREDIT

It is certainly possible to accumulate very large amounts of credit card credit over a short period of time. However, there are some very real drawbacks to this procedure. The worst one is that you will need to find a *very* good investment to pay more in dividends than the interest charged on the cash advances you would take for investment purposes.

Cash advances start accruing interest charges at once, and there is also the cash advance transaction fee which is about 2% of the amount taken. Taken together, these charges can add up to an **effective annual interest rate in excess of 22%**. The other consideration to keep in mind is the **repayment schedule**. Unlike a mortgage, where repayment is amortized over 20 or 30 years, most credit cards base their repayment schedule over 30 to 60 months at the most. If you have $30,000 in cash advances outstanding, the minimum monthly payments can be financially crippling. You might have to repay the money faster than your investment can bear fruit.

Proponents of this supposed wealth-building strategy then say you can trade in the high interest credit card debt for lower interest credit cards and unsecured signature lines of credit from banks. This strategy fails to work as advertised. We have seen that low interest rate credit card issuers are fussy about whom they send cards to. If your credit report reveals that you have $30,000 in credit card debt, it is unlikely that a low rate card issuer will want to do business with you.

The same is true for obtaining signature lines of credit from banks. The credit standards for these lines of credit are very high, and the last thing a bank wants to see on your credit report is an extraordinary level of credit card indebtedness. The other factor to keep in mind is that the rapid exhaustion of these credit card accounts will probably trigger a credit bureau warning program that you are a person who is likely to default.

The key to building borrowing capacity is to develop your credit step by step over time. Schemes for rapid accumulation of massive amounts of unsecured debt are recipes for disaster. Follow the guidelines given in the previous chapters, and within a year you will quality for unsecured credit cards at excellent interest rates. After six months of payment on a secured credit account, apply for a higher interest unsecured credit card. You will probably be approved. Six months later, apply for a lower rate credit card.

CHAPTER 12

AVOIDING DAMAGE TO YOUR CREDIT REPORT

Once you have regained or obtained a favorable credit history, you must take steps to protect it in the future. These steps involve preventing negative information from getting on your credit report and avoiding or minimizing potential credit problems. Millions of people now face such problems due to layoffs or other financial hardships. When financial hardship occurs, the first consideration must be to avoid serious damage to your credit report.

HOW MUCH CREDIT CAN YOU AFFORD?

Many credit problems occur through misuse of credit. This is especially true of those individuals who are new to credit. Problems normally start small, and with little warning. The first step in avoiding credit problems is to understand how much credit you can afford to carry. This figure can be determined easily. Make a list of all your fixed monthly expenses. These include the following:

RENT OR HOUSE PAYMENT

TRANSPORTATION OR CAR PAYMENT

FOOD

TOILETRIES AND SUNDRY ITEMS

INSURANCE

CLOTHING

MISCELLANEOUS MONTHLY EXPENSES

This list will vary somewhat from person to person. The total of these expenses should be subtracted from your net or take home pay each month. The amount of money left over is the theoretical amount of money that could be applied each month to credit payments.

It is a theoretical amount because it assumes that all of your disposable income is committed to credit payments, and that you have no savings. This is a recipe for disaster. Any unforeseen financial crisis will cause a catastrophe. Notice as well that this figure is the amount of credit payments you can *afford*, not the amount of total credit you can *carry*.

As an example, let's assume that you have $500 left over each month. In theory, you could afford a total credit payment of $500 per month. This could be in any combination of credit cards and installment loans. What would happen if suddenly you were temporarily laid off for four months? You would have no savings and would default at once on your credit payments.

At most, **your credit payments should total no more than 40% of your disposable income** after meeting basic obligations. This allows you to build a cushion of savings to absorb financial setbacks. Credit problems often begin with the overuse of credit cards. It starts so slowly, that most people don't even realize it is occurring.

EARLY WARNING SIGNS OF CREDIT PROBLEMS

Credit cards encourage people to spend more. This is one of the lures credit card companies use to encourage merchants to sign up to accept their cards. Credit cards encourage higher levels of spending because they separate us from the transaction. The expenditure becomes an abstraction. No money changes hands, and no check is written. You can purchase $500 worth of merchandise, but your bank balance remains the same. After all, it is the creditor's money that is paying the merchant. Here are some warning signs:

1. YOU ARE TAKING CASH ADVANCES ON YOUR CREDIT CARDS TO PAY OTHER BILLS AND MONTHLY OBLIGATIONS.

2. YOU ARE AT OR NEAR THE LIMIT ON TWO OR MORE OF YOUR CREDIT CARDS.

3. YOU ARE ONLY ABLE TO MAKE THE MINIMUM MONTHLY PAYMENTS ON YOUR CREDIT CARDS.

4. YOUR CREDIT CARD BALANCES ARE ALWAYS INCREASING EACH MONTH.

5. YOU ARE CONSIDERING OBTAINING ANOTHER CREDIT CARD TO PAY OFF THE OLD ONES.

These are the early warning signs of credit trouble. They can be solved if they are dealt with *sooner rather than later.*

DEALING WITH CREDIT PROBLEMS

CONTACT YOUR CREDITORS

The first step is to **contact your creditors to work out alternative arrangements** before you miss a payment. Creditors are very receptive when a borrower contacts them before a problem develops. You will find that most creditors will be very willing to reduce your payment, or to waive payments entirely for a period of time until you are on your feet again. By contacting them early, the creditor feels that you are a responsible person who has hit a rough spot. The creditor also is interested in keeping you as a customer. Make sure that you request that the creditor report the payment arrangement to the credit bureau, and follow up all telephone conversations with a letter confirming the new payment arrangements.

DEBT CONSOLIDATION LOANS

Some people facing large credit card debts, but who are still able to make their minimum payments, consider debt consolidation loans as a possible solution. These loans need to be looked at skeptically by most people. They can cause a person with a manageable problem to deteriorate into a situation where bankruptcy is the only solution.

On the face of it, a debt consolidation loan looks like an excellent idea. High interest credit card debts can be wiped out, and replaced by only a single payment to be made to one creditor. A closer inspection reveals a different result. Most companies that offer these loans are finance companies, not banks and credit unions. Typically, these loans are the first step in a downward financial spiral as a result of simple human nature.

Consider a borrower with an income of $25,000 a year who has $6,000 in credit card debts. The monthly payments are stifling, and the borrower decides to get a bill consolidation loan to reduce the payments. A few weeks later, all of the credit cards are paid off, and in place of four or five payments is a single payment to the finance company. Our borrower notices at once that he has more extra money left over each month.

He also notices that the balances on his credit cards are zero, and like most people, begins to use them again. Within a year, the credit cards are all at the limit again. But now the situation is much worse. Not only must the credit card bills be paid, but the bill consolidation loan payment must also be made. What does he do now? Attempt to get another bill consolidation loan? He may be successful in doing so. The process will then be repeated with the credit cards, but the chances of a third bill consolidation loan are next to nil. Any creditor looking at this borrower's credit report will see what is occurring.

The problem with bill consolidation loans is that they give the *illusion* of wiping out debt, when in reality all that has been done is to transfer the debt from one lender to another. This is why banks shy away from making this type of loan. A very high percentage of people who get these loans later declare bankruptcy. A bill consolidation loan is successful only if the borrower has superhuman discipline. The credit cards must be cut up and thrown away until the consolidation loan has been paid down by at least 50%. Most people are unable to do this.

CONSUMER CREDIT COUNSELING SERVICE

If your credit problems are especially serious, consider using the services of the nonprofit consumer Credit Counseling Service. This agency has offices nationwide and creditors are very familiar with them. They charge no fees to the borrower, and often are able to work out more favorable terms with a creditor than you could on your own. Their national office can direct you to a local office in your area. The address:

CONSUMER CREDIT COUNSELING
8701 GEORGIA AVENUE
SILVER SPRING, MD 20910
1-800-388-2227

When credit problems first occur, be aware that not all creditors report overdue accounts to credit bureaus quickly. Credit card companies and banks will report late payments at once unless alternative payment arrangements are made. However, some creditors will not report late payments until an account is written off. Such creditors include:

TELEPHONE COMPANIES

DOCTORS

LAWYERS

POWER COMPANIES

LANDLORDS

MOST OIL COMPANY CREDIT CARDS

The key to reducing the impact of financial problems with creditors is to take action *before* the situation becomes worse. Contact creditors and work out arrangements. Above all, protect your credit rating.

CHAPTER 13

CHECK VERIFICATION SERVICES

Check verification services have become very popular in the last decade. Many businesses and financial institutions use these services before accepting checks from customers. Banks and credit unions use them before opening new checking accounts for customers. Many consumers have difficulties with these services in the same way they do with credit bureaus. The Fair Credit Reporting Act regulates check verification services as well as credit bureaus. Problems with check verification agencies can be dealt with using methods similar to those outlined for problems with a credit bureau. But first, we need to examine how a typical service operates.

Check verification services allow a merchant to accept checks from customers without a lot of risk. One reason these services grew so rapidly was the outlawing of certain procedures previously used by merchants before accepting a check. Merchants frequently would ask the check writer to show a credit card with the check. The credit card number and expiration date would be written on the check. Some merchants would even run a credit authorization against the credit card for the amount of the check. If a check was returned unpaid, the merchant would then process a credit card sales draft for the amount of the check.

Consumers filed many complaints with consumer protection agencies at the state level against merchants who adopted these practices. The result of these complaints in many states was the outlawing of merchants requesting credit card numbers when accepting a check. The Visa and MasterCard Interbank Associations also made it clear to merchants that they did not have the right to run authorizations or process charge drafts for check purchases.

Even in the age of the credit card, check sales still account for a large percentage of a typical retail store's business. Merchants that stop taking personal checks often experience a drop in sales. Merchants needed a way to continue to accept personal checks while at the same time reducing their exposure. In this respect a check transaction is a credit transaction. Until the check is actually paid to the merchant, no money has changed hands. The check itself can be considered to be equivalent to the promise to repay a credit agreement.

HOW CHECK AUTHORIZATION SERVICES WORK

A check authorization service transfers the risk of nonpayment on a check from the merchant to the check verification service. In return for this assumption of risk, the check verification service requires that the merchant follow certain procedures when accepting a check, that the merchant authorize the check through the service's computer system, and that the merchant pay a certain percentage of the value of each check accepted to the check verification service. This is almost exactly the same arrangement a merchant enters into when becoming a client of the Interbank Associations.

A check verification service operates by constantly building up a database on everyone who comes in contact with it, and a second database of those who run afoul of it. The merchant is usually required to obtain the driver's license number of the customer when a check is presented. Then, using a terminal similar to a credit card authorization machine, the license number, bank account number, check number, and amount of the check are entered into the check service's computer. The computer checks for a match against the "Bad" file of those whose checks are not to be accepted.

If the customer is not in the "Bad" file, an authorization number will be issued and the check accepted by the merchant. On some systems, if the check writer is new to the service, a file will be created using the identifying information gleaned from the check and license. The check service computer will then keep track of the checks that each person writes.

What happens when a check bounces? When this occurs, the individual who bounced the check will have his or her name, license number and state, and bank account number entered into the "Do Not Accept" file. If this person later tries to write a check at a merchant who uses this service, the check will be refused. When a check bounces, the merchant allows the check verification service to handle all communication with the customer.

The check service will send a letter to the consumer informing him or her that the check was returned unpaid and asking that the amount of the check plus a processing fee be remitted. If this is not done within a short period of time, the check service pays the merchant the amount of the check. The check service then initiates collection activity against the check writer. This is one reason merchants happily use these services. It frees them from having to worry about collecting on bounced checks. Essentially the check verification service is selling insurance against unpaid checks to the merchant.

Once a check verification service has an unpaid check on its books, it will take the normal collection activity against the consumer. The service is now also a creditor of the consumer, and will often report this debt to the credit bureau if it is not paid promptly by the consumer.

Banks and credit unions also use these services prior to opening a new checking account. The bank will call the check verification service and give it the name and Social Security Number of the customer. The service will respond with either a yes or a recommendation that an account not be opened. If the answer is no, the bank is not told the reason. The customer whose account is denied must be given a card that has the address and telephone number of the check service. The customer must then call the service to find out why they have a negative file.

DISPUTING NEGATIVE INFORMATION

If you have negative information that is erroneous on file with a check guarantee service, it can be disputed under the Fair Credit Reporting Act in the same manner as with a credit bureau. Some state-level credit reporting agency laws also apply to check verification services. The worst problem with these services for consumers is when negative information is in the files due to financial hardship. If you have attempted to strike a payoff deal with one of these services, but have been unsuccessful, another option exists.

A negative file at a check agency hurts your credit in a unique way. Not only is there the negative entry on your credit report, but you are also prevented from opening a new bank account to re-establish yourself. One way around this is to use a similar method to the file segregation used with credit bureaus.

RE-ENTERING THE SYSTEM

We have seen that the driver's license number or state identity card number is a key part of the system. The first step is to obtain a state identity card from a neighboring state. This can be done easily by obtaining a mailing address in the state, and then making a trip there to get the identity card.

The second step involves either obtaining a genuine new Social Security Number, or changing one digit of your present one. When a bank account is opened, the actual Social Security card is rarely requested. This problem, although slight, can be averted entirely by opening a bank account by mail. Write to banks and credit unions in your home city using your out-of-town mailing address. In the letter state that you need to open an account and would like "bank by mail" supplies. Some banks will refuse to open an account via mail, others will readily agree to do so.

When you fill out the account forms, change a digit in the Social Security Number and also transpose your first and middle names. When the bank checks with the verification service, your name will come back clear. You can now write checks again. You just must remember to always show your out-of-state identification when you present the check. This is often no problem with the guarantee services, as long as the check is imprinted with your name and address.

If you do first attempt to resolve a problem with a check guarantee service, you must negotiate with each service involved, just as with the different credit bureaus. The largest check guarantee service in the United States is Telecheck, but there are others, such as SCAN and CCV. The correspondence from the check service will identify which service is involved.

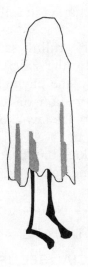

CHAPTER 14

HOW CREDIT BUREAUS INVADE YOUR PRIVACY

You have seen that the credit bureaus are voracious gatherers of information about anyone listed in their files. Most of us assume that this information can be only disclosed when we explicitly make a request for credit. This is far from the case. Credit bureaus are allowed to disclose certain parts of your credit history to anyone at any time.

The credit bureaus do millions of dollars of business a year in selling information from credit reports to third parties that have nothing to do with the granting of credit. This practice was not legal until 1989 when the Federal Trade Commission (FTC) made a narrow ruling on what constitutes "consumer credit data" on a credit report. This ruling created the current wholesale market in selling this personal information.

The FTC ruling said the only information on a credit report that is confidential and protected by the Fair Credit Reporting Act is the actual credit history information itself. Specifically, the payment and balance data submitted by credit grantors to the bureau. The other information on the credit report, commonly called "**Header information**," is not protected by the law and can be given (or sold) to anyone.

What does this header information consist of? Typical header information will contain the following data:

FULL NAME

BIRTHDATE

SOCIAL SECURITY NUMBER

EMPLOYER

POSITION

CURRENT ADDRESS

TWO PREVIOUS ADDRESSES

PREVIOUS EMPLOYER

MARITAL STATUS

This is a *lot* of very personal information. The bureaus package and sell this information as "**Identification**" reports. With a name and an address, the credit bureau computer will search its files for a match and return the information listed above. A second type of header search allows the input of just a Social Security Number and returns the names and addresses of everyone using that particular number (of course only one person should legally have that number, but you'd be surprised…).

Who purchases these identification reports? Private detectives, repo men, attorneys, investigative reporters, direct marketing firms—in short, anyone who wishes to snoop. There are no regulations on who can purchase these reports. No legitimate reason is necessary. The availability of header information has led to the development of **information brokers.** These are companies that contract with each bureau to access their files directly. The information broker then resells this information to its subscribers at a markup.

Unfortunately, nothing can be done to prevent this rape of personal privacy by the credit bureaus. Appendices 7 and 8 show the sales brochures from one credit bureau for two of its identification report products.

Credit bureaus not only violate your privacy, they also do the same thing to your credit report. We have seen how some of the credit bureau warning programs can wrongly label you as a bad credit risk, and there are now so many of these warning programs that a majority of credit reports ordered now contain one or more of these warnings.

The other way the credit bureaus rape your credit is by vastly expanding access to credit reports to those who do not grant credit directly. We will examine this problem in detail in the next chapter.

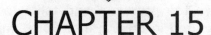

CHAPTER 15

HOW CREDIT BUREAUS RAPE YOUR CREDIT

The credit bureaus have attempted to vastly expand the number of people who have access to your credit report. In many instances, these purchasers do not grant credit themselves, but they still may access your full report. Why do the bureaus do this? Well, it's simple. The credit bureaus' interest is in selling as many credit reports as possible. Each report sold means revenue to the credit bureau.

There was a time when the only businesses that could obtain full credit reports were those that extended credit to customers directly: banks, finance and loan companies, furniture stores, and the like who allowed customers to purchase on terms. Now many noncredit grantors can also order a credit report on *you*. These noncredit grantors include residential landlords, real estate brokers, automobile dealers, and even banks opening checking and savings accounts.

The credit bureaus sold themselves to **residential landlords**, for example, as a way to reduce losses by not renting to tenants who have a poor credit history. **Real estate agents** and **automobile dealers** were told that they could use credit reports as a way to avoid wasting time on prospects who would not later be able to obtain financing.

Real estate agents don't grant credit. They usually have a number of banks to which they refer clients for financing. The same is true of most automobile dealers. With the exception of the small number of used car lots that proudly proclaim, "Buy here, pay here," most automobile dealers do not grant credit directly. They finance customers via the financing arms of the automakers themselves, or through local banks.

Automobile dealers, in fact, are one of the largest sources of credit report abuse. Many times, auto dealers run credit reports on customers without their prior consent. The scam usually operates like this:

> A customer is in the showroom looking at a new car. A salesperson approaches the prospect and talks to him for a while to see if he is really interested in buying a car or is just a browser. If the salesman thinks the prospect is for real, he will offer a test drive or the chance to win a television, or some other prize, if the prospect fills out, say, a contest entry form.
>
> From either the customer's driver's license or the contest entry form, the dealership now has enough information to pull a credit report on the prospect. While the potential customer is out test driving the car, the credit manager pulls the report and determines if the customer can qualify to buy the car.

Not once during this investigation did the customer give his or her consent for a credit report to be ordered. This should be illegal, but it is not. When this specific issue came before the Federal Trade Commission, the auto dealers said that the potential customer was giving his *implicit authorization* to have his credit report pulled. Their reasoning is that very few people can afford to pay cash for a car, so the very act of being in a dealership is tacit approval for a credit report to be run.

Credit bureaus also allow **third party information brokers** access to full credit reports. The information broker is supposed to ensure that the client requesting the credit report has a permissible purpose under the law. Frequently, there is no more than just a nonspecific statement by the client that they have such a purpose. The credit bureau itself is isolated from the abuse of the report because they take the position that it was a subscriber who abused the system, not the credit bureau's lax policies regarding access.

How easy is it for a company or individual to gain access to credit reports via a third party information broker? *Very easy indeed*. In many cases the only documentation required by an information broker is a copy of the company's incorporation papers or fictitious name registration and two references. Often, even less documentation is required.

Remember, every time an inquiry is made on your credit report, it is recorded. Too many inquiries, even unauthorized ones, can result in your being denied credit when you want it or really need it. The more people who have access to your file, the greater the chance of this happening to you.

The credit bureaus have tried to get more **employers** to use credit reports in conjunction with hiring new employees. Under the credit reporting law, employers are entitled to pull credit reports on prospective new employees. In practice, very few companies order credit reports on new workers. A few very large firms do, and many companies of all sizes will run a credit report if the position sought involves a high degree of financial responsibility. An applicant for corporate treasurer or payroll supervisor position might have a report run.

WARNING PROGRAMS

To get more employers to use credit reports in pre-employment screening, bureaus have created new products specifically for employment screening and they are now vigorously advertising these to employers. If the credit bureaus are successful in their efforts, credit reports will be a common part of pre-employment screening in a few years. The attendant risk and damage that inaccurate credit bureau information can have on the individual just grows and grows.

We discussed previously how credit bureaus use risk scoring programs and fraud warning programs on credit reports. These services are sold to credit grantors at an extra cost per report as a way to reduce losses from default. These risk scores are not disclosed to consumers when they request a copy of their reports.

The problem with these programs is that there are now so many of them that nearly *half of all credit reports* contain some warning or a bad risk score. A bad risk score or other warning is often sufficient to cause a creditor to reject your credit request. The following situations can cause a warning to flash on the credit report:

> EXCESSIVE CREDIT INQUIRIES
>
> WRONG SOCIAL SECURITY NUMBER
>
> ADDRESS PREVIOUSLY USED BY BAD DEBTORS
>
> MISSPELLED NAME
>
> MAIL DROP ADDRESS
>
> NONRESIDENTIAL ADDRESS

ANSWERING SERVICE TELEPHONE NUMBER

SOCIAL SECURITY NUMBER NOT ISSUED

DEATH CLAIM SOCIAL SECURITY NUMBER

As is obvious, a simple keystroke error can activate one of these warnings. The more people who have access to your credit report, the greater the chance of an input error causing one of these "black flags" to grace (or disgrace, to be more accurate) your file. Appendix 4 contains a detailed description of some of the warning programs used by major credit bureaus.

There is another loophole in the credit reporting law. This exception allows the credit bureaus to avoid the limitations imposed on them by the law. This is applicable when the amount borrowed is over $50,000, when a job carries an annual salary of $20,000 or more, or when it is what is known as an "Investigative" credit report. The next chapter goes into more detail on these loopholes.

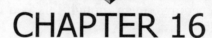

CHAPTER 16

SPECIAL CREDIT REPORTS

Credit bureaus are able to circumvent most of the regulations regarding credit reporting when an investigative credit report is ordered, when the amount of credit to be extended is $50,000 or more, or when the report is in conjunction with a job that pays more then $20,000 per year. These special reports can also be ordered when a life insurance policy in excess of $50,000 has been applied for.

Most people become subject to one of these reports when a mortgage is being sought. Typically, the mortgage processor will obtain reports from all three bureaus on an applicant and compare them. The processor then consolidates the information on all three reports into one in order to get a total picture of the consumer's finances. The special nature of these reports allows the mortgage banker to ask questions not usually posed on a regular credit report. One question mortgage bankers frequently want answered is: What was the source of the downpayment money for the house?

The mortgage banker consults all three reports to determine if the downpayment was obtained via a cash advance on a credit card as opposed to being taken from savings. If it was obtained from a credit card advance, it will probably be considered unfavorably, because it may have increased the total debt load of the applicant beyond acceptable levels.

An **investigative credit report** allows the creditor grantor to make inquiries into the lifestyle and habits of the potential borrower. The law actually defines which characteristics the report is allowed to quantify. They include:

GENERAL CHARACTER

REPUTATION IN COMMUNITY

PERSONAL CHARACTERISTICS

MODE OF LIVING

As is obvious, these qualities are very subjective. To ascertain this information, the credit bureaus dispatch field investigators or hire private detectives to make inquiries. A field investigation normally is ordered only on very large mortgages or life insurance policies that pay over $300,000. These reports can cause a loan applicant to be rejected for something as simple as being in divorce proceedings, even though this is a common situation in the late 1990s.

Someone with an axe to grind can also cause you to lose a job or not get a loan simply on the basis of unfavorable gossip. Technically, under the law, the subject of such a report must be notified no later than three days after the report is ordered. But the law is flaccid even on this point. The disclosure the consumer receives will be a cryptic sentence saying only that an investigative report was prepared and if the consumer wishes more information he or she should write a letter to the address provided. Only after going to the trouble of doing so, and of course with a further delay, will the consumer be able to learn the substance of the report.

Credit bureaus have been successfully sued by consumers for being denied employment or mortgages due to negative information contained in these investigative reports. Such suits must be filed under state laws to have a chance of success, because state laws provide protection that often far exceeds the impotent Federal legislation.

CHAPTER 17

ONLINE CREDIT INFORMATION

The explosive growth of the Internet in the last few years now allows those with credit problems to tap another source of information. There are literally hundreds of sites on the World Wide Web that offer some sort of credit information, as well as numerous newsgroups that have similar topics.

This information is provided by credit bureaus, banks, credit counseling services, consumer groups, trade associations, and private individuals. Some of this information is very accurate and timely, some of it is wrong, and some of it is illegal, or placed there by scam artists hoping to relieve credit-starved people of their hard-earned money.

The key to evaluating any information about credit posted on the Internet is to use caution. Anyone can open up a very nice web site with fancy graphics and post totally false information that appears to be real because it comes across your computer screen. Many of the fancier web sites that purport to offer credit cards to those without good credit are absolute scams, or at the very least, are dubious.

A Nevada corporation was offering a preapproved credit card to anyone who would pony up a $150 annual fee. In return, the individual would receive a "Moneyfirstcard," with a $2,000 line of credit. Most people who responded to this advertisement assumed they were receiving a major bank credit card. The reality was that the card they received was good only to purchase items from a catalog the company also issues.

Although this offer was not a complete fraud, it is at best misleading. I suggest you read the full text of any such offer, because it will make you aware — to be charitable — of one of the popular types of Internet offers typically made to credit-starved individuals.

Appendix 5 contains a series of screen captures from Bank Rate Monitor™ (http://www.Bank Rate.com), a highly useful site for up-to-date financial and credit information.

We discussed in previous chapters the folly of the credit repair agencies. To recap, they have no magical method other than the Fair Credit Reporting Act and various state laws to force credit bureaus to amend the information in their files. To make this clear, a reprint of the Federal law that deals explicitly with what credit bureaus must do to reinvestigate and verify the authenticity of the data in their files is reprinted in Appendix 2. This is the only Federal law that credit repair agencies may use.

On the Internet you will find many credit repair agencies advertising their services, talking about secret methods or secret forms they will sell you. It is all a farce. Many credit repair agencies now do business over the Internet because some states have passed tough new laws that do not allow such agencies to collect money from the customer until after the service has been provided. Locating themselves on the Internet avoids the problem of jurisdiction. A credit repair agency could use a computer based in Europe, Canada, or Mexico, just as easily as they could use a computer located in the United States. Regardless of where a credit repair agency is located—cyberspace or down the block—you can more effectively accomplish the same task by following the procedures outlined in this book.

The Internet sites mentioned so far are excellent sources of up to the minute information on all aspects of consumer credit. Many sites do not charge for access to their sites. The Bank Rate Monitor™ site contains detailed information on credit card rates, specific issuers, and general trends in the credit granting industry.

Many banks and finance companies now allow people to apply online for credit cards. New document encryption schemes allow credit applicants to safely send their personal information over the Internet. Online searching for credit card offers can be a time effective method for an individual who is attempting to expand his or her credit lines, or for individuals who are searching for the very latest in secured credit cards or low interest rate cards.

In a previous chapter we examined special qualification credit cards, such as those issued to college students. New banks are entering this market all the time. The Internet will allow you to locate new issuers in the market quickly. Reprinted in Appendix 9 are some credit card tips (`http://financiallywired/credit_card/tips.html`) from the Internet. Some web sites even allow you to apply for a student card on the Internet.

Big national credit issuers also accept applications over the Internet. Capitol One bank is one of the largest credit card issuers in the United States. Capitol One is not a bank in the traditional sense. They do not have branches, instead they are a credit card bank. Capitol One uses a highly sophisticated credit screening process to determine who should get their cards, based on the likelihood of the individual defaulting. Capitol One is also very aggressive in terminating cardholders who default on other credit accounts they have. More about this in the next chapter.

Capitol One also offers a secured credit card program and information is available about this on their web site (`http://www.capital1.com`). Their unsecured cards should only be applied for if you have established at least a year of solid credit performance on a minimum of three accounts.

The following banks are examples of those that offer online credit card applications:

CAPITOL ONE	`http://www.capital1.com`
DISCOVER CARD	`http://www.discovercard.com`
NATIONSBANK	`http://www.nationsbank.com`
FORT KNOX NATIONAL BANK	`http://fortknoxnational.com/visa/visa.html`
FRANKLIN BANK	`http://www.franklinbank.com`
FIRST WACO NATIONAL BANK	`http://www.fwnb.com`
CHASE MANHATTAN BANK	`http://oneweb.cmb.com/noframes/home.html`
BANK ONE	`http://www.bankone.com`

This listing changes constantly, as more banks offer credit services online. Another popular program is to offer motor vehicle financing online. GMAC, the financing arm of automaker General Motors (`http://www.portchev.com/gmac.html`) now does this in association with local automobile dealers. The credit applicant completes an application on line, which is electronically sent to a nearby dealer for processing. Within about thirty minutes the applicant receives an e-mail voucher if the applicant has been approved. This voucher is then taken to the dealer and presented with the applicant's driver license.

Beginning on the next page appears a reprint out of the Bank Rate Monitor™ site (`http://www.Bank Rate.com`) about auto finance online in general. One advantage to this type of service for people with poor credit is that you can avoid the embarrassment of applying for credit in person and being rejected. If you use one of these services and are rejected, you will receive an e-mail message from the lender stating as much.

There is even a website — staffed mainly by volunteers — named Victims of Credit Reporting (VCR). You'll find this very informative site (see Appendix 10 for proof) at `http://members.aol.com/davevest/vcr.html`.

As you have seen, there are numerous credit-related web sites. The way to locate these sites is to use a search engine, such as Yahoo. Because companies may change their web site addresses, it is best to follow the following procedure to locate appropriate sites, and other credit related Internet web sites.

First, go to Yahoo. The address is: `http:/www.yahoo.com`. Once you are there, type in `"credit repair"`, `"credit cards"`, or other related language in the search box. After you submit the search, you will get back any number of matches. Scroll through these and click on the ones that seem most interesting or appropriate. To locate a specific corporation, simply enter that corporation's name into the search box.

Note also that you can download (for a fee) your personal credit report off the Internet from several credit bureaus. See Appendix 1 for Equifax's offering.

We briefly mentioned that some creditors are using sophisticated credit scoring programs provided with the credit report to accept or reject credit applicants. We will discuss these controversial programs in the next chapter.

Preapproved Auto Loans Making a Splash on the Net ... from Bank Rate Monitor™

N. PALM BEACH — Preapproved auto loans — the kind consumers can take to a dealer and finance with little haggling or hassle — are surfacing more and more on the Internet.

Financial institutions, auto dealers and manufacturers are offering their own spin on auto sales and marketing. Chase, Barnett, GMAC, Community Credit Union and a host of other corporations each have staked a claim in the auto buying process...either in offering preapproved loans or auto purchase information or other options online.

Chase Auto Finance has an exclusive agreement with Auto-By-Tel to provide financing for vehicles purchased through Auto-By-Tel's car-buying service. Barnett, meanwhile, owns Oxford Resources, which offers auto loans through its Car Finance site.

Numerous credit unions and a few small banks have entered the preapproved auto loan market as well. Their loan volume is small compared to in-branch volume, but a presence on the Internet and product awareness are worth the effort, marketing directors said. State Savings Bank in Columbus, Ohio, for example, has been offering auto loans on the Internet since the fourth quarter of 1996.

"We made a decision that we wanted to have as many other types of applications as possible in place on the Internet before we pursued this," said Phil Miller, assistant vp-lending at the $2.6-billion institution. 'This is just one of our many lending avenues online."

Miller said auto loans on the Internet were easy to produce and made the bank very accessible, because it was reaching a market that would allow smaller outfits to have equal billing with the bigger banks.

"The demographics of the Internet was the kind we wanted to go after for bank loans," Miller said. "We wanted the younger, affluent, better-educated consumers. This was the ideal kind of person we wanted to go after."

One of the drawbacks of the system in place now is that State Savings Bank's branch system is in central Ohio, and loans must be completed at one of its branches.

"If we get an application from Pennsylvania, the only way to service it is to come to Columbus and service it here, and we have closed some loans," Miller explained. "We view the auto loans as a marketing tool for our other products, as well. If they look at us in that regard, maybe they will look at us in some other regard. We can pull them into some other areas and offer our products."

The preapproved State Savings Bank loans have garnered "limited success," Miller added. "We're talking about closing one or two loans a month, with 24-hour turnaround for the client, but for the price and the effort we had to put into it, we have more than paid for the website."

Miller and other lenders who offer preapproved auto financing on the Internet believe they take the pain out of the car-buying process. "Purchasing a car is intimidating to most, and our preapproved system makes the loan process less expensive for both the consumer and the bank," he said.

In a recent speech by Consumer Bankers Association Reports, Steven LaMore, president of Barnett Dealer Finance Services Inc. in Jacksonville, Fla., said the auto superstores, their captive finance companies and the use of the Internet to buy and finance cars was "moving auto loans out of the realm of traditional lenders."

However, Barnett has already moved into the arena of preapproved auto loans, via its recent purchase of Oxford Resources, which created two websites about two months ago that offer autos and preapproved financing: http:/www.priceautooutlet.com/pao/ and http:www.carfinance.com/fin/. Financing is available through either site, but users can view auto pricing details only at the Price Auto Outlet site.

Electronic Vehicle Remarketing Inc. (EVRI) in Melville, N.Y. is the division of Oxford that handles its Internet business. Through Price Auto Outlet, customers can purchase a car in [any of] five states and have the auto shipped to their doorstep. It is important to note that the financing provided is not limited to the five-state region, but is available nationwide.

At Car Finance, payment quotes are available and customers, typically those with A or B-type credit, can qualify for pre-approved loans. When approval is met, they are notified by email and can print out the message as a voucher for the loan.

"There aren't very many preapproved loans like ours on the Internet," said Bob Ferber, president of EVRI. "We are different from other sites in that we don't focus on dealer relationships. We give the customers quotes and the preapproval for a loan and they can present that to any dealer…it is not restricted to just a few dealers in our network, and that is what is critical."

Dealers try to recoup revenues lost in a sale by massaging the financing in their favor, Ferber said — by charging a higher interest rate or adding other costs to the final financing.

"We are working to eliminate the abuse," Ferber said. "You get that real good price, and you're ready to do the financing, and suddenly, you find the deal is not quite as attractive as it once was. You're all ready to go and they hit you with their package…the dealers can make up their lost gross profit on financing."

The Oxford Resources voucher system, which is offering consumers a variety of auto loans, allows consumers the ability to present financing in advance, Ferber said. At this time, Oxford is cuffing the loan and lease rates by *50* basis points for Internet users, creating another marketing edge.

"People hate the sales finance pressure at the dealership," Ferber added. "We don't want to take anything away from the dealer. We see this as an expansion of their customer base."

Thus far, the site has experienced tremendous activity, he noted. "We're getting about 25,000 page views per day and taking a couple hundred applications per day."

Oxford recently added a new loan to its mix — the College Graduate Auto Loan — which provides auto loan financing to new graduates who may or may not have credit. "All we ask is that there is no derogatory credit and you must be employed in your field upon graduation," explained Phil Bouren, retail credit executive for Barnett Dealer Financial Services Inc. in Melville, N.Y., which provides the loan products for the Car Finance site.

The new preapproved loan product focuses on selling or leasing used cars to college graduates, since this is the optimum time of year to reach that target audience. "Making auto loans is something we have done for a long, long time and we have always concentrated on A and B credit," Bouren said. "We're not taking tremendous risks. We see the Internet as an opportunity and it is a wide open, untapped market for us.
Bouren is cautious about talking about results as yet. "It is so early in the process and we are still testing it and still learning a lot. We drive the customer there. We want to sign up that dealer and book that contract, so that he then becomes part of our large network of dealers. He is still very much involved in the financing process.

While Oxford is integrating its financial products with Barnett Dealer Financial Services, and is sharing resources, technically, the loan is held by Oxford.

"So far we have thousands of dealers in five states signed up with us," Bouren said. "It's a formality at this point."

The process promises 48-hour loan approval but it usually takes less time than that, Bouren said. "We provide lots of customer support. There is an 800 number on the voucher they receive from our system, and we have a full-time staff on hand to answer any questions. We view this as a viable venture, not just an experiment. We are closing loans."

Auto manufacturer competitors have offered these types of preapproved loan products on the Internet, but work within a specific manufacturer's dealer network, such as GM, Toyota and Ford.

"We put our shortened credit application on the Internet last Fall, but before we did, we put a forum on the Internet," said Mike McFall, assistant director of communications for GMAC in Detroit. "The consensus was that it would speed up the process at the dealership and give the consumer some empowerment in the process. So far, the response to our Internet applications has been very favorable."

GMAC now has a system in place that notifies those who apply online within a couple of minutes, McFall said, about whether or not their loan has been approved. Two things happen, he added. A message is faxed to the dealer that this customer has applied and approved. Then, a preapproved certificate is mailed to the customer.

"'To prevent abuses of the system, we send it by mail, thereby eliminating the potential for fraud and abuse'" McFall said. "That is not necessarily a forward-thinking perspective, but it is the right thing to do. We feel it is just too easy to appropriate content and repurpose it."

The dealer can verify the authenticity of the preapproval with GMAC by using a toll-free number, so the buyer can potentially go to the dealer the moment the approval flashes on his computer screen.

"We had limited expectations of this system's success, and it has exceeded those expectations," McFall said. "This preapproval process is great for everyone, because it identifies the credit-worthy up front. We are working now to make it faster and better."

Even if the customer is denied a preapproved loan, information is sent to a dealer, who may examine the application and call the customer to work out another type of financing arrangement, McFall said. "Just because you don't get instant approval does not mean you can't get a lease or loan. The dealers typically work with the customers."

Another group that is working with providing auto financing through both credit unions and banks is CUC International Inc. in Stamford, Conn. This company owns Auto Vantage, a website that provides an auto buying service with about 3,000 dealers in the network.

Digital Insight is partnering with CUC to put Auto Vantage's information on credit union sites and provide Auto Vantage links for other sites.

Scoff Ciccari, who operates CUC's Credit Union Auto Vantage program, said 10 credit unions are linked to Auto Vantage's home page and the company is working on site incorporations with others. Community Credit Union in Plano, Texas is one of its members and is involved in a test pilot of the branded site, designed by Digital Insight.

"Auto Vantage offers new car summaries on Community Credit Union's site, in its 'online services section'," Ciccari explained. "The car buying services are built right into their site. Customers can click onto a preapproval form, send it and then we refer them to a dealer. It's a common cliché', but we call it 'no haggle, no-hassle car buying'."

CUC is partnering this project with Digital Insight, which in turn has formed relationships with roughly 130 financial institutions to provide its auto buying information on their sites. These institutions pay a one-time set up fee in exchange for customer referrals from Auto Vantage. Customers can view car summary guides online and request pricing on a desired auto. Once they decide to make the purchase, the loan application is available online through the institution.

Kathi Cavanagh, home banking coordinator at Community Credit Union, explained the relationship this way;

"Digital Insight created the Auto Vantage site within our site, a process we call 'branding it' to our site. We pay Digital Insight for the Auto Vantage information on our site, which they are offering as an additional option at a cost. There is no cost for the referrals back and forth from Auto Vantage, because we are part of a test pilot of this system."

Once on Community Credit Union's site, the first step that appears is the loan application online from the CU. Turnaround time is one to two days.

The second option is the Auto Vantage listing of cars with consumer information and photos, etc., Cavanagh said. And the third option on the page is dealer contact or dealer referral with a "preferred price," provided by Auto Vantage.

"So far, we have taken 10 applications for auto loans and closed one loan," Cavanagh said. "I think it will take a while for it to catch on. But we believe this is an added convenience for our members to have the loans, the cars and the dealers right there on our site."
Community Credit Union auto loans are priced on a tiered basis. For a new loan up to 60 months, the average rate is 7.75 percent. The $440-million CU offers no discount for Internet users.
CUC is enthusiastic about the future success of its site affiliations.

"If linking your site to Auto Vantage increases your auto loans by two loans a month, that pays for the arrangement," Ciccari said. "We want to change the way cars are bought and sold in this country."

CHAPTER 18

CONTROVERSIAL SCREENING PROGRAMS

We have seen that creditors maximize their profits by charging as much in interest and fees as the marketplace will allow, and also by minimizing credit losses due to chargeoffs, bankruptcies, or outright fraud. Creditors are using two methods to accomplish this. These procedures are vital to the new generation of credit card issuers in particular.

Traditional banks issue credit cards in addition to many other liens of business. A typical bank makes money from the difference in interest it pays on deposit accounts — checking and savings — and the interest it receives from lending out these same funds in the form of automotive, business, credit card, and mortgage loans. Traditional banks also collect millions of dollars a year in income from service charges levied on most accounts.

This diversified source of income means that a loss in one area of banking income may be offset by profits elsewhere. The new generation of national credit card issuers do not have this diversified source of income.

Credit card lending can generate massive profits. The ideal credit card customer is an individual who earns a good, steady income, pays his bills on time, and will carry a large balance on his credit card for a number of months before paying it off. This individual will generate a steady stream of profits in the form of interest charges on his unpaid balance.

The cost of servicing this customer is minimal. He requires no expensive branches with their associated personnel costs. He requires only a small piece of plastic and monthly statements. A bank that did away with all other types of services, and only issued credit cards to this type of individual could create massive profits.

The problem is locating this individual to whom to extend credit. The downside to this type of banking is that if your credit card holders start to default, there is no offsetting income from other lines of business. So absolute control of defaults is necessary.

RISK SCORES

The credit bureaus responded to this challenge by offering what are called risk scores on credit reports provided to creditors. For an extra fee, each credit report ordered from the bureau will have a risk score. This analysis is supposed to predict the likelihood that the card applicant will become a chargeoff or go into bankruptcy.

These programs use a number of variables to make this determination:

TOTAL NUMBER OF REVOLVING CREDIT ACCOUNTS

TOTAL CREDIT AVAILABLE ON ALL REVOLVING ACCOUNTS

TOTAL BALANCE OUTSTANDING

ANNUAL INCOME

PAYMENT HISTORY

RATE OF CREDIT LINE USAGE

NUMBER OF NEW ACCOUNTS OPENED IN LAST YEAR

NUMBER OF CREDIT INQUIRIES

What these programs do is take all of these variables, and then compare them with a computer model of people who become deadbeats. A score is generated, usually between 300 and 1000. The higher the score, the more desirable the applicant. Each creditor determines its own cutoff scores, but the computer model comes with recommendations. Some creditors have gone so far as to only request the score from the credit bureau, and no longer even review the credit report.

This can be very troublesome for an individual who has one charged off account that was a legitimate dispute, but otherwise has a spotless credit report. The risk analysis program may very well assign this individual an unacceptable score, and cause rejection. Some mortgage lenders are now starting to request these scores on reports as well.

These programs will look at how much available credit you have at your disposal. This will be compared against your income level. Creditors who use this system say that it is a valid concern, because you could go out and charge all of your credit cards to their theoretical maximum, and then default.

The rate at which you go through credit lines is supposed to be another predictor of possible bankruptcy. If the computer analysis shows that you typically max out a $5,000 credit card in six to eight months, a future prediction may show that in three or four years your total debt to income ratio will be equal to that of typical bankrupts.

The problem with this is that any number of factors could account for such use of credit lines. A medical emergency, or even a decision to return to school in midcareer, could both cause someone to start using credit lines more aggressively. An individual who has just lost his job might need to supplement his reduced income with credit card cash advances until another job is found.

Capitol One uses this scoring system aggressively. This allows them to offer large credit lines to creditworthy individuals. However, you can be denied even if you are creditworthy and fall outside the parameters of the scoring system.

One applicant for a Capitol One account was a technical professional in Southern California. The individual concerned had received his doctorate two years earlier. He had numerous student loans and other installment debt typical of someone who has spent an extended time in academia. His payment history was spotless. However…

Capitol One rejected his application, because even though his income level was high now, he had too many other debts to be considered.

One way around this problem is to request a **balance transfer** when you apply for one of these cards. These issuers will always ask if you want to pay off a higher rate card with a balance transfer when you apply for their card. If you agree to do this, many of these issuers will approve the account, even if you would have been rejected for already having too much available credit. A balance transfer tells them you will not be increasing your total indebtedness, and may cause them to approve the account.

If you have good credit and are turned down by one of the issuers who rely upon these risk scoring models, you may be able to get the decision reversed by **calling the credit department after you receive the rejection letter**. At that point your credit history will be reviewed by an individual, and you will have an opportunity to make your side of the story known. Quite often you will be approved after this review, but with a lower credit line than before.

Another caution is that as your risk score declines, you become a worse risk, as each inquiry is made into your credit history. Automobile dealers are notorious for abusing credit reports. Dealers will typically "shop" a car loan to a few different lenders they work with. This is especially true with used car dealers who do not maintain a relationship with the financing arms of one of the major automakers.

When your loan application reaches, say four different lenders used by the dealer, each of them will pull a credit report. These lenders don't typically use the risk analysis software, so they could care less about your risk score. You purchase the car, and assume that it is done.

Six months later you apply for a credit card from a lender who does use risk analysis, and you are declined. You are declined because your risk score was heavily affected by the four inquiries made on your credit report the day you purchased the car.

Always ask how many inquiries will be made on your credit history before going through with any credit application.

These new generation credit card lenders do not only use risk analysis *proactively*, before they grant you credit, they also use it *retroactively* once you are a cardholder. This can result in your account being cancelled or your credit line reduced with no prior warning to you.

Credit card issuers have always had the right to request updated credit reports on their customers. Typically, this was only done if a current card member in good standing requested a very large increase in their credit line. Customers who paid their bills on time usually did not have new credit reports pulled.

The new generation issuers will pull credit reports on their cardholders annually, and it is not done to approve large increases in credit lines. It is done to see if a current cardholder has become a less desirable credit risk over the last year. If the consumer's risk score has declined below acceptable levels, the full credit report will be ordered. As we have seen, any number of reasons can cause a less desirable risk score. Your card might be cancelled because you have opened a new credit card account, or were late paying some bills.

Some issuers use these as pretexts when they are trying to reduce their exposure to certain parts of the country or even certain types of employment. One national issuer did this a few years ago during the recession with certain account holders who lived in the Industrial Northeast, which was hit hard during the recession.

There is not a thing you can do about lenders who utilize these systems. In the fine print on your credit card agreements, you will see that all creditors reserve their right to monitor your credit reports. One issuer goes so far as to require new cardholders to promise in writing not to open any new credit card accounts when they receive their new card.

CHAPTER 19

NEW DEVELOPMENTS

The world of credit is constantly changing. Some of these changes are beneficial to the consumer, but many are harmful to their interests. The first topic we will look at is a relatively new service that can be very useful if you are using the dispute strategy to remove negative and erroneous information from your credit report.

This service, called **Confidential Credit,** summarizes the information contained in the credit reports maintained by the big three credit bureaus. The report costs $26 plus shipping and handling. One nice aspect of the Confidential Credit report format is that it reports the information more in the format that real credit reports are issued in. This is especially true in the case of Experian (formerly known as TRW). The TRW credit report that is issued to consumers bears no resemblance to what a credit grantor receives. It is a verbal summary of each item on the report.

The Confidential Credit report ranks account payment status according to the previously detailed industry system, and clearly shows what bureau is reporting what information.

When you dispute an item, you still must dispute each item with the bureau that is reporting it, not with Confidential Credit. In Appendix 3 is a reproduction of an Consumer Credit Report Sample. As you can see, it is very clear and detailed. You can order a copy by calling: 1-800-442-4879. I still suggest you order a copy of your report from each of the three main bureaus after you have used the Confidential Credit Report to clean up your credit files. Errors can occur whenever data is transferred from one file to another.

On the legal front, the news is also mixed. A few states are considering tougher legislation regulating credit bureaus, but to date, only Massachusetts has passed new laws to give consumers more power in credit bureau disputes.

The flip side of this is that Congress has been considering new Federal laws to regulate the bureaus. These new laws, although somewhat stronger than the existing Federal legislation, come nowhere close to having the teeth of some of the proposed new state laws.

The credit bureaus, in an attempt to keep their regulatory environment as unfettered as possible, are lobbying Congress intensely for a compromise. The large bureaus will agree not to oppose the new Federal laws, if the Federal laws will supercede all state legislation. This issue is far from being resolved.

If you are forced to initiate a legal dispute with a credit bureau, and you live anywhere but Massachusetts, your best bet is to go through Small Claims Court unless you can get an attorney to take your case on a contingency basis.

The credit bureaus destroy most plaintiffs by dragging out what is known as the **discovery process**. During this procedure the credit bureau attorneys will question the plaintiff extensively about all sorts of financial records, most of which have little or no bearing on the dispute at hand. All the while, hundreds of dollars an hour in attorney fees are accruing to the plaintiff. This becomes prohibitively expensive very quickly. The amount of damages you can collect in Small Claims Court are limited, but your chances of prevailing are much greater.

Another tactic would be to **obtain a mailing address in Massachusetts**, and apply for credit with this address. Once you have been rejected, you now can avail yourself of the very strong Massachusetts credit reporting laws. The Massachusetts statutes allow consumers to collect substantial damages, and to apply for injunctive relief, which forces the bureau to stop reporting the disputed information until it is settled at trial, and other effective remedies.

Massachusetts is probably the most active state in trying to protect consumer's rights in credit transactions. It even has its own website

http://www.boston.com/crashpad/hood/ccreditc.htm

For a sample of their highly useful information, see Appendix 11.

Another tactic credit bureaus have been using recently is to threaten consumers who dispute items with correspondence that contains warnings to the effect that a **frivolous dispute** is a Federal crime and other such language. Do not be intimidated by such words. The law gives you specific rights, and you cannot be prosecuted for availing yourself of them.

Credit bureaus are now making it harder to get **good information added to credit reports**, unless it comes from a subscribing creditor. One easy way to get positive payment information added to your credit report used to be via magazine subscriptions, book and record clubs, health clubs that bill monthly, and like businesses.

Experian (formerly known as TRW) has stopped accepting these types of establishments as subscribing creditors, although they may continue to report delinquent or charged off accounts to the bureau. At the same time, Experian is aggressively expanding its search for information on consumers who are not yet in their files.

Experian owns associated corporations that collect information on life insurance applicants, and is negotiating agreements with utility companies, such as local telephone service and electricity companies, to send customer information to them. This way they can create files on consumers who have made a conscious decision to stay out of the credit game.

Finally, **third party access to your credit report** has been vastly expanded. Third party access to credit information occurs anytime someone other than a credit grantor, landlord, or employer directly accesses your credit report.

It used to be very difficult for a third party to gain access to credit reports unless they first agreed to a lengthy vetting process by the bureau. The only time this did not happen was when the third party was clearly involved in consumer finance, such as automobile dealers or real estate firms.

Now, information resellers, called *information brokers*, have access to credit bureau files. These information brokerage companies specialize in compiling information from any number of sources, and then reselling the results to their customers.

A few of these firms require customers who want access to consumer credit reports to completed documentation as to why they need this access, and tag each report ordered with the customer's business name. This practice is far from universal.

Many information brokers will sell credit reports to any customer, as long as the customer signs a pro forma statement that he or she has a permissible reason to request the report under the Fair Credit Reporting Act. The credit bureaus are not concerned about the abuse this can cause because it simply means they are selling more product.

The ultimate goal of the credit bureaus is to get *everyone* into their system. That is why credit bureaus also operate debt collection subsidiaries and some even operate check approval services. All of this information about consumers finds its way into their files, even if no credit has been applied for.

APPENDIX 1

CBI/CSC CREDIT REPORT

(EQUIFAX)

EQUIFAX CREDIT REPORT LEGEND

CURRENT MANNER OF PAYMENT (Using Payments Past Due Or Age from Due Date)	TYPE O	OF R	ACCOUNT I
Too new to rate; approved but not used	0	0	0
Pays (or paid) within 30 days of payment due dale. **Or** not over one payment past due	1	1	1
Pays (or paid) in more than 30 days from the payment due date. Bill not more than 60 days. **Or** not more than two payments past due	2	2	2
Pays (or paid) in more than 60 days from payment due date. Bill not more than 90 days. **Or** three payments past due	3	3	3
Pays (or paid) in more than 90 days from payment due date. but not more than 120 days, **Or** four payments past due	4	4	4
Pays (or paid) in more than 120 days **Or** more than four payments past due	5	5	5
Making regular payments under debtor's plan **Or** similar arrangement	7	7	7
Repossession. (Indicate if it is a voluntary return of merchandise by the consumer)	8	8	8
Bad debt	9	9	9

CODE	MEANING
I	Individual Account. The subject of the report, and no one else. Is responsible for payment on this account.
J	Joint Account. The subject and another person (or other persons) are jointly responsible for payment on this account.
A	Authorized Use. This is a shared account, but one person has responsibility for payment, while the other person (or other persons) does not.
U	Undesignated. This code is an indication that the credit grantor does not have enough information to give the account a more specific designator code.
S	Shared, but otherwise undesignated. This code is an indication that the credit grantor knows that the subject and at least one other person share the account, but not enough information is available to designate the account as either "J" (Joint) or "A" (Authorized Use).
C	Co-maker. The subject has co-signed for an installment loan, and will be responsible for payment if the borrower should default.
M	Maker. The subject is responsible for payment of an installment loan, but a co-maker is involved as assurance that the loan will be repaid.
B	On Behalf of Another Person. The subject has financial responsibility for an account which is used exclusively by another person, as when a father opens a charge account for his daughter's use at college.
T	Terminated. The subject's relationship to this account has ended, although other parties who once shared the account with the subject may continue to maintain the account. This code is used often after a divorce, when one party continues to maintain an account while the other party is disassociated from it.

TYPE OF ACCOUNT
I = Installment
0 = Open
R = Revolving

INDUSTRY CODES

A AUTOMOTIVE
AN Automobile Dealer, New
AU Automobile Dealers, Used
AT TBA Stores, Tire Dealers
AP Automotive Parts
AR Automotive Repair, Body Shops
AS Service Stations
AL Truck Dealers
AF Farm Implement Dealers
AZ Miscellaneous

B BANKS
BB Banks

C CLOTHING
CG General Clothing Stores
CS Specialty, Shoes, Hats, etc.
CZ Miscellaneous

D DEPT. & VARIETY
DC Complete Dept stores
DV Variety Stores
DM Mail Order Firms
DZ Miscellaneous

F FINANCE
FA Auto Financing
FF Sales Financing
FP Personal Loan Co.
FM Mortgage Co.
FS Savings & Loan Assoc.
FC Credit Unions
FZ Miscellaneous

G GROCERIES
GD Dairies
GN Neighborhood Grocer
GS Supermarkets
GZ Miscellaneous

H HOME FURNISHINGS
HA Appliance Sales/Service
HC Carpets & Floor Coverings
HF Furniture, etc.
HM Music & Records
HT Television & Radio
HZ Miscellaneous

I INSURANCE
IG General Insurance
IL Life Insurance
IZ Miscellaneous

J JEWELRY & CAMERAS
JA Jewelers
JC Cameras
JZ Miscellaneous

K CONTRACTORS
KG General
K1 1 Home Improvements
KS Sub-Contractors
KZ Miscellaneous

L LUMBER BLDG.
MATERIALS & HARDWARE
LA Air Conditioning, Plumbing
     Electrical Sales/Service
LF Fixture & Cabinet Co.
LH Hardware Stores
LP Paint, Glass & Paper
LV Lumber Yards
LZ Miscellaneous

M MEDICAL & HEALTH
MB Dentists
MC Chiropractors
MD Doctors & Clinics
MF Funeral Homes, Cemeteries
MH Hospitals
MO Osteopaths
MP Pharmacies & Drugs
MS Optometrists, etc.
MV Veterinarians
MZ Miscellaneous

O OIL & NAT'L CREDIT CARDS
OC Oil Companies
ON National Credit Card Co:
OZ Miscellaneous

P PERSONAL SERVICES
PA Accountants, etc.
PB Barber / Beauty Shops
PD Dry Cleaning, Laundry
PE Engineering. All Kinds
PG Photographer.
P1 Legal & Related Services
PZ Miscellaneous

R REAL ESTATE, HOTELS, ETC.
RA Apartments
RE Real Estate. Sales/Rent
RH Hotels
RM Motels
RZ Miscellaneous

S SPORTING GOODS
SB Boat & Marinas. Sales/Service
SG Sporting Good Stores
SM Motorcycles & Bicycles. Sales
     and Service
SZ Miscellaneous

T FARM & GARDEN SUPPLIES
TC Chemical & Fertilizer Stores
TF Feed & Seed Stores
TN Nursery & Landscaping
TZ Miscellaneous

U UTILITIES
UC Coal & Wood Dealers
UD Garbage & Rubbage Disposals
UE Electric Light & Power
UF Fuel Oil Dealers
UG Gas, Natural & Bottled
UT Telephone Co.
UW Water Co.
UZ Miscellaneous

V GOVERNMENT
VC City & County
VF Federal
VS State
VZ Miscellaneous

W WHOLESALE
WA Automotive Supplies
WB Bldg. Supplies & Hardware
WC Clothing & Dry Goods
WD Drugs & Chemicals
WG Groceries & Related Products
WH Home Furnishings
WM Machinery & Equipment
WZ Miscellaneous

X ADVERTISING
XA Agencies
XM News Media
XZ Miscellaneous

Y COLLECTION SERVICES
YA ACB of A
YC Others

Z MISCELLANEOUS
ZB Reporting Agencies
ZR Retail, not elsewhere classified
ZS Services not elsewhere
ZW Wholesale, not elsewhere
ZX CBR
ZY CSI
ZZ All Others-Business
     Machines, Catering, Vending
     Machines, Schools, Aircraft
     Leasing, Railroads, Clubs.
     Lodges, Shopping Centers.
     Travel Agencies

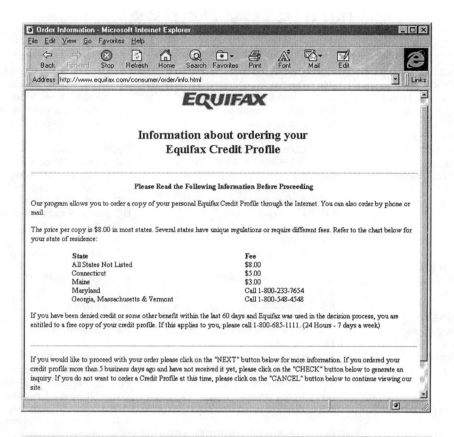

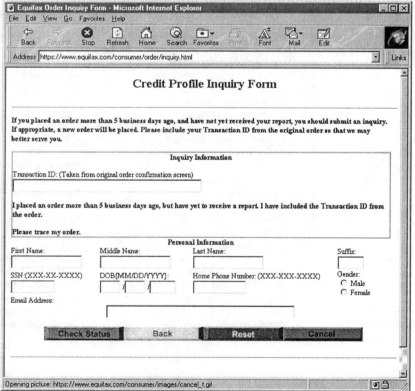

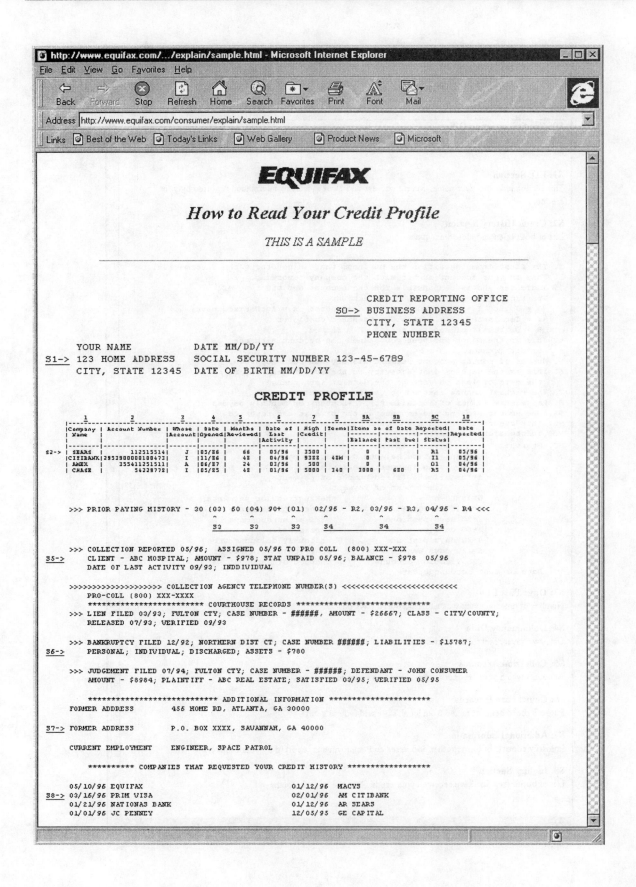

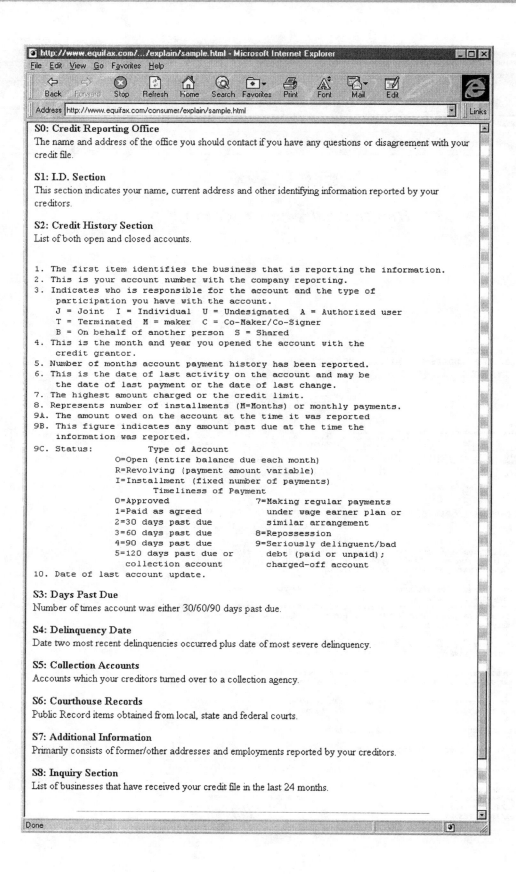

http://www.equifax.com/.../explain/sample.html - Microsoft Internet Explorer

File Edit View Go Favorites Help

Address http://www.equifax.com/consumer/explain/sample.html

S0: Credit Reporting Office

The name and address of the office you should contact if you have any questions or disagreement with your credit file.

S1: I.D. Section

This section indicates your name, current address and other identifying information reported by your creditors.

S2: Credit History Section

List of both open and closed accounts.

```
1. The first item identifies the business that is reporting the information.
2. This is your account number with the company reporting.
3. Indicates who is responsible for the account and the type of
   participation you have with the account.
   J = Joint   I = Individual   U = Undesignated   A = Authorized user
   T = Terminated   M = maker   C = Co-Maker/Co-Signer
   B = On behalf of another person   S = Shared
4. This is the month and year you opened the account with the
   credit grantor.
5. Number of months account payment history has been reported.
6. This is the date of last activity on the account and may be
   the date of last payment or the date of last change.
7. The highest amount charged or the credit limit.
8. Represents number of installments (M=Months) or monthly payments.
9A. The amount owed on the account at the time it was reported
9B. This figure indicates any amount past due at the time the
    information was reported.
9C.  Status:         Type of Account
                O=Open (entire balance due each month)
                R=Revolving (payment amount variable)
                I=Installment (fixed number of payments)
                     Timeliness of Payment
                0=Approved              7=Making regular payments
                1=Paid as agreed           under wage earner plan or
                2=30 days past due         similar arrangement
                3=60 days past due      8=Repossession
                4=90 days past due      9=Seriously delinguent/bad
                5=120 days past due or     debt (paid or unpaid);
                   collection account      charged-off account
10. Date of last account update.
```

S3: Days Past Due

Number of times account was either 30/60/90 days past due.

S4: Delinquency Date

Date two most recent delinquencies occurred plus date of most severe delinquency.

S5: Collection Accounts

Accounts which your creditors turned over to a collection agency.

S6: Courthouse Records

Public Record items obtained from local, state and federal courts.

S7: Additional Information

Primarily consists of former/other addresses and employments reported by your creditors.

S8: Inquiry Section

List of businesses that have received your credit file in the last 24 months.

Done

APPENDIX 2

THE FAIR CREDIT REPORTING ACT

THE FAIR CREDIT REPORTING ACT

TITLE VI—PROVISIONS RELATING TO CREDIT REPORTING AGENCIES

AMENDMENT OF CONSUMER CREDIT PROTECTION ACT

SEC.601.   The Consumer Credit Protection Act is amended by adding at the end thereof the following new title.

"TITLE VI—CONSUMER CREDIT REPORTING

SEC.
Section 601   Short Title.
Section 602   Findings and Purpose.
Section 603   Definitions end Rules of Construction.
Section 604   Permissible Purposes of Reports.
Section 605   Obsolete Information.
Section 606   Disclosure of Investigative Consumer Reports.
Section 607   Compliance Procedures.
Section 608   Disclosures to Governmental Agencies.
Section 609   Disclosures to Consumers.
Section 610   Conditions of Disclosure to Consumers.
Section 611   Procedure in Case of Disputed Accuracy.
Section 612   Charges for Certain Disclosures.
Section 613   Public Record Information for Employment Purposes.
Section 614   Restrictions on Investigative Consumer Reports.
Section 615   Requirements on Users of Consumer Reports.
Section 616   Civil Liability for Willful Noncompliance.
Section 617   Civil Liability for Negligent Noncompliance.
Section 618   Jurisdiction of Courts: Limitation of Actions.
Section 619   Obtaining Information under False Pretenses.
Section 620   Unauthorized Disclosures by Officers or Employees.
Section 621   Administrative Enforcement.
Section 622   Relation to State Laws.

§ Short title

"This title may be cited as the Fair Credit Reporting Act.

§602. Findings and purpose.

(a) The Congress makes the following findings:

(1) The banking system is dependent upon fair and accurate credit reporting. Inaccurate credit reports directly impair the efficiency of the banking system, and unfair credit reporting methods undermine the public confidence which is essential to the continued functioning of the banking system.

(2) An elaborate mechanism has been developed for investigating and evaluating the credit worthiness, credit standing, credit capacity, character, and general reputation of consumers.

(3) Consumer reporting agencies have assumed a vital role in assembling and evaluating consumer credit and other information on consumers.

(4) There is a need to insure that consumer reporting agencies exercise their grave responsibilities with fairness, impartiality, and a respect for the consumer's right to privacy.

(b) It is the purpose of this title to require that consumer reporting agencies adopt reasonable procedures for meeting the needs of commerce for consumer credit, personnel, insurance, and other information in a manner which is fair and equitable to the consumer, with regard to the confidentiality, accuracy, relevancy, and proper utilization of such information in accordance with the requirements of this title.

§603. Definitions and rules of construction

(a) Definitions and rules of construction set forth in this section are applicable for the purposes of this title.

(b) The term "person" means any individual, partnership, corporation, trust, estate, cooperative, association, government or governmental subdivision or agency, or other entity.

(c) The term "consumer" means an individual.

(d) The term "consumer report" means any written, oral, or other communication of any information by a consumer reporting agency bearing on a consumer's credit worthiness, credit standing, credit capacity, character, general reputation, personal characteristics, or mode of living which is used or expected to be used or collected in whole or in part for the purpose of serving as a factor in establishing the consumer's eligibility for (1) credit or insurance to be used primarily for personal, family, or household purposes, or (2) employment purposes, or (3) other purposes authorized under section 604. The term does not include: (A) any report containing information solely as to transactions or experiences between the consumer and the person making the report; (B) any authorization or approval of a specific extension of credit directly or indirectly by the issuer of a credit card or similar device; or (C) any report in which a person who has been requested by a third party to make a specific extension of credit directly or indirectly to a consumer conveys his decision with respect to such request, if the third party advises the consumer of the name and address of the person to whom the request was made and such person makes the disclosures to the consumer required under section 615.

(e) The term "investigative consumer report" means a consumer report or portion thereof in which information on a consumer's character, general reputation, personal characteristics, or mode of living is obtained through personal interviews with neighbors, friends, or associates of the consumer reported on or with others with whom he is acquainted or who may have knowledge concerning any such items of information. However, such information shall not include specific factual information on a consumers credit record obtained directly from a creditor of the consumer or from a consumer reporting agency when such information was obtained directly from a creditor of the consumer or from the consumer.

(f) The term "consumer reporting agency" means any person which, for monetary fees, dues, or on a cooperative nonprofit basis, regularly engages in whole or part in the practice of assembling or evaluating consumer reports to third parties, and which uses any means or facility of interstate commerce for the purpose of preparing or furnishing consumer reports.

(g) The term "file", when used in connection with information on any consumer, means all of the information on that consumer recorded and retained by a consumer reporting agency regardless of how the information is stored.

(h) The term "employment purposes" when used in connection with a consumer report means a report used for the purpose of evaluating a consumer for employment, promotion, reassignment or retention as an employee.

(i) The term "medical information" means information or records obtained, with the consent of the individual to whom it relates, from licensed physicians or medical practitioners, hospitals, clinics, or other medical or medically related facilities.

§604. Permissible Purposes of Reports

(a) A consumer reporting agency may furnish a consumer report under the following circumstances and no other:

(1) In response to the order of a court having jurisdiction to issue such an order.

(2) In accordance with the written instructions of the consumer to whom it relates.

(3) To a person which it has reason to believe—

A) intends to use the information in connection with a credit transaction involving the consumer on whom the information is to be furnished and involving the extension of credit to, or review or collection of an account of, the consumer; or

(B) intends to use the information for employment purposes; or

(C) intends to use the information in connection with the underwriting of insurance involving the consumer; or

(D) intends to use the information in connection with a determination of the consumer's eligibility for a license or other benefit granted by a governmental instrumentality required by law to consider an applicant's financial responsibility or status; or

(E) otherwise has a legitimate business need for the information in connection with a business transaction involving the consumer.

§605. Obsolete Information

(a) Except as authorized under subsection (b), no consumer reporting agency may make any consumer report containing any of the following items of information:

(1) Cases under Title 11 or under the Bankruptcy Act that, from the date of entry of the order for relief or the date of adjudication, as the case may be, antedate the report by more than 10 years.

(2) Suits and judgments which, from date of entry, antedate the report by more than seven years or until the governing statute of limitations has expired, whichever is the longer period.

(3) Paid tax liens which, from date of payment, antedate the report by more than seven years.

(4) Accounts placed for collection or charged to profit and loss which antedate the report by more than seven years.

(5) Records of arrest, indictment, or conviction of crime which, from date of disposition, release, or parole, antedate the report by more than seven years.

(6) Any other adverse item of information which antedates the report by more than seven years.

(b) The provisions of subsection (a) of this section are not applicable in the case of any consumer credit report to be used in connection with—

(1) a credit transaction involving, or which may reasonably be expected to involve, a principal amount of $50,000 or more;

(2) the underwriting of life insurance involving, or which may reasonably be expected to involve, a face amount of $50,000 or more; or

(3) the employment of any individual at an annual salary which equals, or which may reasonably be expected to equal $20,000 or more.

§606. Disclosure of Investigative Consumer Reports

(a) A person may not procure or cause to be prepared an investigative consumer report on any consumer unless—

(1) it is clearly and accurately disclosed to the consumer that an investigative consumer report including information as to his character, general reputation, personal characteristics, and mode of living, whichever are applicable, may be made, and such disclosure (A) is made in a writing mailed, or otherwise delivered, to the consumer, not later than three days after the date on which the report was first requested, and (B) includes a statement informing the consumer of his right to request the additional disclosures provided for under subsection (b) of this section or

(2) the report is to be used for employment purposes for which the consumer has not specifically applied.

(b) Any person who procures or causes to be prepared an investigative consumer report on any consumer shall, upon written request made by the consumer within a reasonable period of time after the receipt by him of the disclosure required by subsection (a)(l) of this section, make a complete and accurate disclosure of the nature and scope of the investigation requested. This disclosure shall be made in a writing mailed, or otherwise delivered, to the consumer not later than five days after the date on which the request for such disclosure was received from the consumer or such report was first requested, whichever is the later.

(c) No person may be held liable for any violation of subsection (a) or (b) of this section if he shows by a preponderance of the evidence that at the time of the violation he maintained reasonable procedures to assure compliance with subsection (a) or (b) of this section.

§607. Compliance Procedures

(a) Every consumer reporting agency shall maintain reasonable procedures designed to avoid violations of Section 605 and to limit the furnishing of consumer reports to the purposes listed under Section 604. These procedures shall require that prospective users of the information identify themselves, certify the purposes for which the information is sought, and certify that the information will be used for no other purpose. Every consumer reporting agency shall make a reasonable effort to verify the identity of a new prospective user and the uses certified by such prospective user prior to furnishing such user a consumer report. No consumer reporting agency may furnish a consumer report to any person if it has reasonable grounds for believing that the consumer report will not be used for a purpose listed in Section 604.

(b) Whenever a consumer reporting agency prepares a consumer report it shall follow reasonable procedures to assure maximum possible accuracy of the information concerning the individual about whom the report relates.

§608. Disclosures to Governmental Agencies

Notwithstanding the provisions of Section 604, a consumer reporting agency may furnish identifying information respecting any consumer, limited to his name, address, former addresses, places of employment, or former places of employment, to a governmental agency.

§609. Disclosures to Consumers

(a) Every consumer reporting agency shall, upon request and proper identification of any consumer, clearly and accurately disclose to the consumer:

(1) The nature and substance of all information (except medical information) in its files on the consumer at the time of the request

(2) The sources of the information; except that the sources of information acquired solely for use in preparing an investigative consumer report and actually used for no other purpose need not be disclosed: *Provided*, that in the event an action is brought under this title, such sources shall be available to the plaintiff under appropriate discovery procedures in the court in which the action is brought.

(3) The recipients of any consumer report on the consumer which it has furnished—
   (A) for employment purposes within the two-year period preceding the request, and
   (B) for any other purpose within the six-month period preceding the request.

(b) The requirements of subsection (a) respecting the disclosure of sources of information and the recipients of consumer reports do not apply to information received or consumer reports furnished prior to the effective date of this title except to the extent that the matter involved is contained in the files of the consumer reporting agency on that date.

§610. Conditions of Disclosure to Consumers

(a) A consumer reporting agency shall make the disclosures required under section 609 during normal business hours and on reasonable notice.

(b) The disclosures required under section 609 shall be made to the consumer –

(1) in person if he appears in person and furnishes proper identification; or

(2) by telephone if he has made a written request, with proper identification, for telephone disclosure and the toll charge, if any, for the telephone call is prepaid by or charged directly to the consumer.

(c) Any consumer reporting agency shall provide trained personnel to explain to the consumer any information furnished to him pursuant to Section 609.

(d) The consumer shall be permitted to be accompanied by one other person of his choosing, who shall furnish reasonable identification. A consumer reporting agency may require the consumer to furnish a written statement granting permission to the consumer reporting agency to discuss the consumer's file in such person's presence.

(e) Except as provided in Sections 616 and 617, no consumer may bring any action or proceeding in the nature of defamation, invasion of privacy, or negligence with respect to the reporting of information against any consumer reporting agency, any user of information, or any person who furnishes information to a consumer reporting agency, based on information disclosed pursuant to Section 609, 610, or 615, except as to false information furnished with malice or willful intent to injure such consumer.

§611. Procedure in Case of Disputed Accuracy

(a) If the completeness or accuracy of any item of information contained in his file is disputed by a consumer, and such dispute is directly conveyed to the consumer reporting agency by the consumer, the consumer reporting agency shall within a reasonable period of time reinvestigate and record the current status of that information unless it has reasonable grounds to believe that the dispute by the consumer is frivolous or irrelevant. If after such reinvestigation such information is found to be inaccurate or can no longer be verified, the consumer reporting agency shall promptly delete such information. The presence of contradictory information in the consumer's file does not in and of itself constitute reasonable grounds for believing the dispute is frivolous or irrelevant.

(b) If the reinvestigation does not resolve the dispute, the consumer may file a brief statement setting forth the nature of the dispute. The consumer reporting agency may limit such statements to not more than one hundred words if it provides the consumer with assistance in writing a clear summary of the dispute.

(c) Whenever a statement of a dispute is filed, unless there is reasonable grounds to believe that it is frivolous or irrelevant, the consumer reporting agency shall, in any subsequent consumer report containing the information in question, clearly note that it is disputed by the consumer and provide either the consumer's statement or a clear and accurate codification or summary thereof.

(d) Following any deletion of information which is found to be inaccurate or whose accuracy can no longer be verified or any notation as to disputed information, the consumer reporting agency shall, at the request of the consumer, furnish notification that the item has been deleted or the statement, codification or summary pursuant to subsection (b) or (c) of this section to any person specifically designated by the consumer who has within two years prior thereto received a consumer report for employment purposes, or within six months prior thereto received a consumer report for any other purpose, which contained the deleted or disputed information. The consumer reporting agency shall clearly and conspicuously disclose to the consumer his rights to make such a request. Such disclosure shall be made at or prior to the time the information is deleted or the consumer's statement regarding the disputed information is received.

§612. Charges for Certain Disclosures

A consumer reporting agency shall make all disclosures pursuant to section 609 and furnish all consumer reports pursuant to section 611 (d) without charge to the consumer if, within thirty days after receipt by such consumer of a notification pursuant to section 615 or notification from a debt collection agency affiliated with such consumer reporting agency stating that the consumer's credit rating may be or has been adversely affected, the consumer makes a request under section 609 or 611 (d). Otherwise, the consumer reporting agency may impose a reasonable charge on the consumer for making disclosure to such consumer pursuant to section 609, the charge for which shall be indicated to the consumer prior to making disclosure; and for furnishing notification, statements, summaries, or codifications to person designated by the consumer pursuant to section 611(d), the charge for which shall be indicated to the consumer prior to furnishing such information and shall not exceed the charge that the consumer reporting agency would impose on each designated recipient for a consumer report except that no charge may be made for notifying such persons of the deletion of information which is found to be inaccurate or which can no longer be verified.

§613. Public Record Information for Employment Purposes

A consumer reporting agency which furnishes a consumer report for employment purposes and which for that purpose compiles and reports items of information on consumers which are matters of public record and are likely to have an adverse effect upon a consumer's ability to obtain employment shall-
(1) at the time such public record information is reported to the user of such consumer report, notify the consumer of the fact that public record information is being reported by the consumer reporting agency, together with the name and address of the person to whom such information is being reported; or
(2) maintain strict procedures designed to insure that whenever public record information which is likely to have an adverse effect on a consumer's ability to obtain employment is reported it is complete and up to date. For purposes of this paragraph, items of public record relating to arrests, indictments, convictions, suits, tax liens, and outstanding judgments shall be considered up to date if the current public record status of the item at the time of the report is reported.

§ 614. Restrictions on Investigative Consumer Reports

Whenever a consumer reporting agency prepares an investigative consumer report, no adverse information in the consumer report (other than information which is a matter of public record) may be included in a subsequent consumer report unless such adverse information has been verified in the process of making such subsequent consumer report, or the adverse information was received within the three-month period preceding the date the subsequent report is furnished.

§615. Requirements on Users of Consumer Reports

(a) Whenever credit or insurance for personal, family, or household purposes, or employment involving a consumer is denied or the charge for such credit or insurance is increased either wholly or partly because of information contained in a consumer re port from a consumer reporting agency, the user of the consumer report shall so advise the consumer against whom such adverse action has been taken and supply the name and address of the consumer reporting agency making the report.

(b) Whenever credit for personal, family, or household purposes involving a consumer is denied or the charge for such credit is increased either wholly or partly because of information obtained from a person other than a consumer reporting agency bearing upon the consumer's credit worthiness, credit standing, credit capacity, character, general reputation, personal characteristics, or mode of living, the user of such information shall, within a reasonable period of time, upon the consumer's written request for the reasons for such adverse action received within sixty days after learning of such adverse action, disclose the nature of the information to the consumer. The user of such information shall clearly and accurately disclose to the consumer his right to make such written request at the time such adverse action is communicated to the consumer.

(c) No person shall be held liable for any violation of this section if he shows by a preponderance of the evidence that at the time of the alleged violation he maintained reasonable procedures to assure compliance with the provisions of subsections (a) and (b)

§616. Civil Liability for Willful Noncompliance

Any consumer reporting agency or user of information which willfully fails to comply with any requirement imposed under this title with respect to any consumer is liable to that consumer in an amount equal to the sum of—

(1) any actual damages sustained by the consumer as a result of the failure;

(2) such amount of punitive damages as the court may allow; and

(3) in the case of any successful action to enforce any liability under this section, the costs of the action together with reasonable attorney's fees as determined by the court.

§617. Civil Liability for Negligent Noncompliance

Any consumer reporting agency or user of information which is negligent in failing to comply with any requirement imposed under this title with respect to any consumer is liable to that consumer in an amount equal to the sum of—

(1) any actual damages sustained by the consumer as a result of the failure;

(2) in the case of any successful action to enforce any liability under this section, the costs of the action together with reasonable attorney's fees as determined by the court.

§618. Jurisdiction of Courts: Limitation of Actions

An action to enforce any liability created under this title may be brought in any appropriate United States district court without regard to the amount in controversy, or in any other court of competent jurisdiction, within two years from the date on which the liability arises, except that where a defendant has materially and willfully misrepresented any information required under this title to be disclosed to an individual and the information so misrepresented is material to the establishment of the defendant's liability to that individual under this title, the action may be brought at any time within two years after discovery by the individual of the misrepresentation.

§619. Obtaining Information Under False Pretenses

Any person who knowingly and willfully obtains information on a consumer from a consumer reporting agency under false pretenses shall be fined not more than $5,000 or imprisoned not more than one year, or both.

§620. Unauthorized Disclosures by Officers or Employees

Any of officer or employee of a consumer reporting agency who knowingly and willfully provides information concerning an individual from the agency's files to a person not authorized to receive that information shall be fined not more than $5,000 or imprisoned not more than one year, or both

§621. Administrative Enforcement

(a) Compliance with the requirements imposed under this title shall be enforced under the Federal Trade Commission Act by the Federal Trade Commission with respect to consumer reporting agencies and all other persons subject thereto, except to the extent that enforcement of the requirements imposed under this title is specifically committed to some other government agency under subsection (b) hereof. For the purpose of the exercise by the Federal Trade Commission of its Actions and powers under the Federal Trade Commission Act, a violation of any requirement or prohibition imposed under this title shall constitute an unfair or deceptive act or practice in commerce in violation of Section 5(a) of the Federal Trade Commission Act and shall be subject to enforcement by the Federal Trade Commission under Section 5(b) thereof with respect to any consumer reporting agency or person subject to enforcement by the Federal Trade Commission pursuant to this subsection, irrespective of whether that person is engaged in commerce or meets any other jurisdictional tests in the Federal Trade Commission Act. The Federal Trade Commission shall have such procedural, investigative, and enforcement powers, including the power to issue procedural rules in enforcing compliance with the requirements imposed under this title and to require the filing of reports, the production of documents, and the appearance of witnesses as though the applicable terms and conditions of the Federal Trade Commission Act were part of this title. Any person violating any of the provisions of this title shall be subject to the penalties and entitled to the privileges and immunities provided in the Federal Trade Commission Act as though the applicable terms and provisions thereof were part of this title.

(b) Compliance with the requirements imposed under this title with respect to consumer reporting agencies and persons who use consumer reports from such agencies shall be enforced under –

(1) section 8 of the Federal Deposit Insurance Act in the case of—

(A) national banks by the Comptroller of the Currency;

(B) member banks of the Federal Reserve System (other than national banks), by the Federal Reserve Board and

(C) banks insured by the Federal Deposit Insurance Corporation (other than members of the Federal Reserve System), by the Board of Directors of the Federal Deposit Insurance Corporation.

(2) section 5 (d)of the Home Owners Loan Act of 1933, section 407 of the National Housing Act, and sections 6 (i) and 17 of the Federal Home Loan Bank Act, by the Federal Home Loan Bank Board (acting directly or through the Federal Savings and Loan Insurance Corporation), in the case of any institution subject to any of those provisions;

(3) the Federal Credit Union Act, by the Administrator of the National Credit Union Administration with respect to any Federal credit union;

(4) the Acts to regulate commerce, by the Interstate Commerce Commission with respect to any common carrier subject to those Acts;

(5) the Federal Aviation Act of 1958, by the Civil Aeronautics Board with respect to any air carrier or foreign air carrier subject to that Act; and

(6) the Packers and Stockyards Act, 1921 (except as provided in Section 406 of that Act), by the Secretary of Agriculture with respect to any activities subject to that Act.

(c) For the purpose of the exercise by any agency referred to in subsection (b) of this section of its powers under any Act referred to in that subsection, a violation of any requirement imposed under this title shall be deemed to be a violation of a requirement imposed under that Act. In addition to its powers under any provision of law specifically referred to in subsection (b) of this section, each of the agencies referred to in that subsection may exercise, for the purpose of enforcing compliance with any requirement imposed under this title any other authority conferred on it by law.

§622. Relation to State Laws

This title does not annul, alter, affect, or exempt any person subject to the provisions of this title from complying with the laws of any state with respect to the collection, distribution, or use of any information on consumers, except to the extent that those laws are inconsistent with any provision of this title, and then only to the extent of the inconsistency. "

EFFECTIVE DATE

SEC.602.Section 504 of the Consumer Credit Protection Act is amended by adding at the end thereof the following new subsection:

"(d) Title VI takes effect upon the expiration of one hundred and eighty days following the date of its enactment."

Approved October 26, 1970.

APPENDIX 3:

EXPERIAN

(FORMERLY KNOWN AS TRW)

experían

CONSUMER CREDIT REPORT SAMPLE

Experian is the independent company formed from TRW's information services businesses.

This is your consumer identification number. Please refer to this number when you call or write us. ID# 1234567890

JONATHON QUINCY CONSUMER
10655 NORTH BIRCH STREET
BURBANK, CA 91502

HOW TO READ THIS REPORT:

An explanatory enclosure accompanies this report. It describes your credit rights and other helpful information. If the enclosure is missing, or you have questions about this report, please contact the office listed on the last page. As part of our fraud-prevention program, account numbers may not fully display on this report.

YOUR CREDIT HISTORY:

This information comes from public records or from organizations that have granted credit to you. An asterisk by an account indicates that this item may require further review by a prospective creditor when checking your credit history. If you believe any of the information is incorrect, please let us know. For your convenience, instructions for reinvestigation are included on the last page of this report.

Experian includes the following statement in all reports of your credit history.

My identification has been used without my permission on applications to obtain credit. Verbal confirmation from me at 805-969-9601 or 123-456-7890 is requested prior to credit approval.

ACCOUNT	DESCRIPTION
1. * US BKPT CT MD 101 W LOMBARD ST BALTIMORE MD 21002 DOCKET #08511002	Voluntary bankruptcy chapter 13 discharged on 05/23/92. Petition on 06/01/90. Recorded assets: $100,000 Liabilities: $8,000. You are solely responsible for this public record item
2. * HOPKINS COUNTY COURT MADISON CNTY CT HOUSE MADISONVILLE KY 4211 DOCKET #2005355267 BK PG SEQ #1386520381	Small claims judgment satisfied on 02/23/93. Original filing date 06/28/92. Amount: $4,100 Plaintiff: Wilson and McPherson. You have joint responsibility for this public record item
.3 * LEE CO CIVIL COURT P O BOX 408 FT MYERS FL 33403 CERTIFICATE # 211412123 BK PG SEQ #	County tax lien on 12/08/91 Amount: $2,000. You are solely responsible for this public record item
4 * WELLS FARGO BANK P O BOX 2096 CONCORD CA 94520 BANKING ACCT # 200543445667XXXX	This credit card account was opened 02/05/91 and has revolving repayment terms. You have contractual responsibility for this account and are primarily responsible for its payment. Credit limit: $5,000.

AS OF 02/22/94, THIS CLOSED ACCOUNT WAS CURRENT AND ALL PAYMENTS WERE MADE ON TIME. BALANCE: $0 ON 04/30/94. MONTHS REVIEWED = 59.

*** ACCOUNT CLOSED-CONSUMER'S REQUEST-REPORTED BY SUBSCRIBER.

5 * CHEMICAL BANK JERICO QUADRANG NY 11753 BANKING ACCT # 456920095206XXXX	This credit card account was opened 05/04/79 and has revolving 300 repayment terms. You have contractual responsibility for JERICO this account and are primarily responsible for its Credit payment. Limit: $3,500, high balance: $2,512.

AS OF 12/15/95, THIS OPEN ACCOUNT IS 120 DAYS 2+ TIMES PAST DUE. BALANCE: $1,695 ON 12/15/95. SCHEDULED MONTHLY PAYMENT IS $73. MONTHS REVIEWED = 99.

```
PAYMENT    44332211CCCCC      CCC-CCCCCCCC    999999999999 999999999666
HISTORY:   5443221111CC       CCCCCCCCCCCC    CCCCCCCCCCC
```

NUMBER OF TIMES LATE: 30 DAYS = 6, 60 DAYS = 4, 90+ DAYS = 11, DEROG = 21.

YOUR CREDIT HISTORY WAS REVIEWED BY:

The following inquiries are reported to those who ask to review your credit history.

INQUIRY	DESCRIPTION
6. CELLULAR ONE 651 GATEWAY PL. SAN FRANCISCO CA 94082 UTILITIES	07/24/95 Inquiry made for credit extension, review or other permissible purpose.
7. METROPOLITAN NATL BK 406 8TH STREET OAKLAND CA 94206 FINANCE.	06/15/95 Inquiry made for real estate loan for 30 years repayment terms. The amount is $200,000. This inquiry was made on behalf of ABC Mortgage

The following inquiries are **not** reported to those who ask to review your credit history. They are included so you have a complete list of inquiries.

INQUIRY	DESCRIPTION
8. EXPERIAN P O BOX 2103 ALLEN TX 75013 UNDEFINED FIRM TYPE #9877333456789023	06/20/95 Inquiry made for consumer disclosure of your credit history.

PLEASE HELP US HELP YOU:

At **Experian** we know how important your good credit is to you. It's equally important to us that our information be accurate and up to date. Listed below is the information you gave us when you asked for this report. If this information is not correct, or you did not supply us with your full name, address for the past five years, social security number and year of birth, this report may not be complete. If this information is incomplete or not accurate, please let us know.

YOUR NAME:	JONATHON QUINCY CONSUMER	SOCIAL SECURITY #:	526603388
ADDRESS:	10655 NORTH BIRCH ST BURBANK CA 91502	YEAR OF BIRTH:	1951
OTHER ADDRESSES:	8 PARK AVE., HUDSON NH 03051	SPOUSE:	SUSAN

IDENTIFICATION INFORMATION:

The following additional information has been provided to us by organizations that report information to us.

Social Security #:	526103388 526603388	REPORTED 3 TIMES REPORTED 6 TIMES
Addresses:	1314 SOPHIA LANE SANTA ANA CA 92708	GEOGRAPHICAL CODE = 123-4632-7

This single-family dwelling address was first reported 11-93 and last reported 12-95 by update. Last reported by Chemical Bank. Address reported 11 times.

Employers: AJAX HARDWARE
               LOS ANGELES CA 90019

FIRST REPORTED 6-94 AND LAST REPORTED 6-95 BY INQUIRY. LAST REPORTED BY METROPOLITAN NATL BK.

Other: Year of Birth: 1941
               Name: CONSUMER, JONATHAN
                                  CONSUMER, JON Q

               Spouse: PATRICIA

FROM 02/01/94 THE NUMBER OF INQUIRIES WITH THIS SOCIAL SECURITY # =5

FACS+ TRANSPORTATION SERVICE ON FACS+ FILE/LUX TRANS/10655 N BIRCH ST/BURBANK CA 91502

SOCIAL SECURITY NUMBER YOU GAVE WAS ISSUED: 1950-1953

* * * END OF THE REPORT * * *

THIS IS YOUR CONSUMER IDENTIFICATION
NUMBER. PLEASE REFER TO THIS NUMBER   ID# 1234567890
WHEN YOU CALL OR WRITE US.

JONATHON QUINCY CONSUMER   SS# 526603388
10655 NORTH BIRCH STREET   YEAR OF BIRTH: 1951
BURBANK, CA 91502   SPOUSE: SUSAN

Reinvestigation Request

We will reinvestigate any item you believe is inaccurate, unless the dispute is frivolous or irrelevant. Just a reminder, a credit report is a history of how accounts were paid; therefore, even a paid collection would not be deleted. Missed payments and most public record items remain on the credit report for seven years, except Chapter 7, 11 and 12 bankruptcies which remain for 10 years. You may complete this form and mail it to the following address:

Experian, P.O. Box 2106, Allen, TX 75013-9506.
For faster service, please call us at 1.800.422.4879
Monday through Friday from 7:30 a.m. to 7:00 p.m. Central Standard Time.

We will contact the source of the information you questioned. When we complete our reinvestigation process, we will send you an updated credit report. You will hear from us again within 30 days of receipt of your request. For us to reinvestigate an item, we need all of the following information:

Social Security number: _____

Company Name:_____   Company Name:_____
Account #: _____   Account #: _____

☐ Not my account   ☐ Never paid late   ☐ Not my account   ☐ Never paid late
☐ Included in my bankruptcy   ☐ Paid in full   ☐ Included in my bankruptcy   ☐ Paid in full

Other: (please explain) _____   Other: (please explain) _____
_____   _____
_____   _____

Company Name:_____   Company Name:_____
Account #: _____   Account #: _____

☐ Not my account   ☐ Never paid late   ☐ Not my account   ☐ Never paid late
☐ Included in my bankruptcy   ☐ Paid in full   ☐ Included in my bankruptcy   ☐ Paid in full

Other: (please explain) _____   Other: (please explain) _____
_____   _____
_____   _____

At your request, we will send the results of our reinvestigation to organizations who reviewed the credit report within the past six months (12 months for residents of MD, NY and VT) or to employers who inquired within the past two years. Please indicate your choices:

_____   _____

_____   _____

CONSUMER CREDIT REPORT (CDI) P-1001 A10T05 11/15/96 14:50:17

Home Page | Experian Products | Customer Service Center | About Us | Site Map
Personal Credit Pavilion | Real Estate Realm | Revolving Showcase | Skyway to Loans
Small Business Credit Cafe | Newsroom | Member Area | Visitors Center | Search Web Site

Experian Webmaster

CREDIT REPORT REQUEST LETTER

Date

Dear sir:

Please send me a copy of my credit report. Enclosed is a check for the necessary fee or a copy of a credit denial letter. My personal particulars are given below.

My full name:_____

My birthdate:_____

My social security number:_____

My present address:_____

_____

My previous address:_____

_____

My telephone number:_____

Thank you,

Signature

THE TRW CREDIT PROFILE REPORT

With input from our subscribers, the TRW Credit Profile report was designed in an easy-to-read format. Information has been included which will enhance your decision-making capabilities. Similar data elements are grouped together so you can analyze data faster.

Files on nearly 170 million credit active consumers nationwide are maintained in the TRW database. Your inquiry initiates a search of this database which produces an applicant's credit history—the TRW Credit Profile report. An illustration and description of a sample Profile report are shown in this brochure.

1. A code which identifies the **TRW or Credit Bureau office** nearest to the consumer's current address. Use for consumer referrals.

2. Consumer's **name and address** as recorded on automated subscriber tapes, including date of most recent update.

3. Consumer's **Social Security Number**.

4. Consumer's **year of birth.**

5. **Spouse's first name initial.**

6. **Employer's name and address** as reported via a subscriber inquiry as of the date shown.

7. **FACS + Summary:** contains messages related to the FACS + fraud prevention services.

8. Message which displays if a consumer's Social Security Number has not been issued or if the number is not valid, based on a check of Social Security Administration records.

9. The number of previous inquiries using this consumer'' Social Security Number within the last four months. **Optional**.

10. The number of previous inquiries using this consumer's current address within the last four months. **Optional**.

11. The **nonresidential** type of **establishment**, address and telephone number displays if a consumer's address matches an address listed in TRW's file of nonresidential addresses.

12. **The Profile Summary**: contains 16 significant calculations from the Profile report. **Optional**.

13. The total number of public record items.

14. Total installment loan account balance owed by the consumer.

15. Total real estate loan balance owed by the consumer.

16. Total revolving charge account balance owed by the consumer.

17. Total dollar amount of past due payments owed by the consumer.

18. The combined total of scheduled and estimated monthly payments owed by the consumer.

19. Total dollar amount of real estate payments owed by the consumer.

20. Total percentage of revolving credit still available to the consumer.

NOTE: An **asterisk** following any Profile Summary total indicates not all trade lines had an amount which could be included in the total.

21. Total NUMBER OF Inquiries.

22. Total of inquiries made within six moths preceding the date of the Profile report.

23. Total number of trade lines on the Profile report.

24. Total of accounts which have been paid satisfactory or paid after having been previously delinquent.

25. Total of accounts which are current or paid satisfactory.

26. Total of accounts which are delinquent or derogatory.

27. Total of accounts which were delinquent or derogatory, and either have been paid in full, or brought current.

28. The date the oldest trade line on the report was opened.

29. **Risk model score**: generated if you use one of TRW's credit risk models. **Optional**.

30. **Score factors**: codes which contributed to the risk model score generated if you use one of TRW's credit risk models. **Optional**.

31. **Public record**: court name, case number filing date, plaintiff, code, amount and type of public record. Public record information consists of bankruptcies, liens, and judgments against a consumer.

32. An **asterisk** preceding public record information or a trade lie indicates that information may need further review.

33. Reporting **subscriber's name**.

34. Consumer's **account number.**

35. Reporting **subscriber's identification number**.

36. **Type** of account.

37. **Terms** of account.

38. Code describing **consumer's association** to the account per the Equal Credit Opportunity Act.

39. **Date** the account was **opened**.

40. **Balance date**: the date balance information was extracted from the subscriber's accounts receivable file.

41. **Date** of consumer's **last payment** on the account.

42. The **amount** of the loan or credit established.

43. Indicates if the amount is an original loan (**O**), credit limit (**L**), high balance (**H**), or charge-off (**C**).

44. **Current balance** of the account.

45. **Monthly payment amount** the consumer is scheduled to pay each month on the account. **Note**: a scheduled monthly payment is indicated if there is no qualifying character directly after the amount.

46. **Estimated monthly payment amount**: indicated by the qualifying character "E" directly after the monthly payment amount.

47. **Status date**: the date the account status was reported to TRW.

48. The **amount past due** for the account.

49. **Account status** comments indicate the payment condition of the account as of the status date.

50. The **consumer's payment history** during the past 24 months. The codes reflect the status of the account for each month and are displayed for balance reporting subscribers only.

C:	Current
N:	Current account/zero balance reported
1:	30 days past the due date
2:	60 days past the due date
3:	90 days past the due date
4:	120 days past the due date
5:	150 days past the due date
6:	180 days past the due date
—(Dash)	No history reported for that month
Blank	No history maintained; see account status comment.

51. **Inquiries**: indicate a Profile report was received by the subscriber listed. Inquiring subscriber, account number, date of inquiry and subscriber identification number are shown. Type, terms and amount may display and are from the subscriber's inquiry input for that particular report.

52. **Profile report messages:** display certain differences between consumer identifying information supplied in the inquiry and information in the database.

53. Name, address and telephone number of **TRW office or Credit Bureau** nearest to the consumer's current address. Use for consumer referrals. **Optional.**

THE TRW CREDIT PROFILE REPORT MESSAGES

CHECKPOINT > > SSN NOT ISSUED AS OF 08/87
This Checkpoint message appears on the Profile report if the applicant's Social Security Number has not been issued as of the date displayed in the message. In general, Checkpoint messages alert you to pertinent information about specific applicant identifiers. When you see a Checkpoint message, you may want to further investigate the information supplied by the applicant.

CHECKPOINT > > SS# IS 524479971
A Checkpoint Variation message will appear when the information in TRW's file relating to the applicant's Social Security Number, generation or year of birth does not correspond to the information entered in the subscriber's inquiry. **It is possible that the information may not pertain to the individual inquired upon.**

CHECKPOINT > >* * * AKA SEARCH * * * LAST NAME IS SMITH
The AKA Search enhancement is designed to automatically retrieve and display additional consumer data associated with alternative surnames—such as aliases, misspelled names and maiden or previous surnames. **It is possible that the information may not pertain to the individual inquired upon.**

CHECKPOINT> >* * * NICKNAME SEARCH * * * 1ST NAME IS BOB
The Nickname Search enhancement includes a Nickname Table containing alternative first names which may be used by an individual. This Nickname Table is automatically referenced for each inquiry and searches with both the given name and the nickname to retrieve additional credit information on an individual. **It is possible that the information may not pertain to the individual inquired upon.**

- - - - -*ATTN* FILE VARIATION: MID INIT IS J
A File Variation message will appear when there are variations in minor identifiers in TRW's file relating to the applicant's middle initial, spouse initial, street initial, last three digits of the zip code or the second and third characters of the first name. **It is possible that the information may not pertain to the individual inquired upon.**

- - - - -FILE INDENT: MID INIT IS Q
A File indent message will appear when information is not given on input, but exists on file.

CAUTION THE ABOVE REPORT MAY CONTAIN ITEMS FOR OTHER MEMBERS OF THE SAME FAMILY
This message may appear when names and addresses are similar. It means that closer checking of the application or with the applicant may be necessary. **It is possible that the information may not pertain to the individual inquired upon.**

****AUTO-FILE—CONTAINS AUTOMATED SUBSCRIBER INFORMATION ONLY****
This message indicates geographic areas which, in general, contain data received from national companies. Local credit grantor and public record information is not yet available.

CONSUMER STATEMENT
TRW Credit Data will accommodate statements on the Profile report in accordance with the Fair Credit Reporting Act and state reporting law.

APPENDIX 4:

CREDIT REPAIR

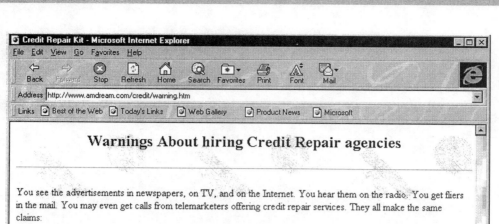

Warnings About hiring Credit Repair agencies

You see the advertisements in newspapers, on TV, and on the Internet. You hear them on the radio. You get fliers in the mail. You may even get calls from telemarketers offering credit repair services. They all make the same claims:

- "Credit problems? No problem!"
- "We can erase your bad credit -- 100% guaranteed."
- "Create a new credit identity -- legally."
- "We can remove bankruptcies, judgments, liens, and bad loans from your credit file forever!"

Do yourself a favor and save some money, too. Don't believe these statements. Only time, a conscious effort, and a personal debt repayment plan will improve your credit report.

If you decide to respond to a credit repair offer, beware of companies that:

- Want you to pay for credit repair services before any services are provided;
- Do not tell you your legal rights and what you can do -- yourself -- for free;
- Recommend that you not contact a credit bureau directly; or
- Advise you to dispute all information in your credit report or take any action that seems illegal, such as creating a new credit identity. If you follow illegal advice and commit fraud, you may be subject to prosecution.

You could be charged and prosecuted for mail or wire fraud if you use the mail or telephone to apply for credit and provide false information. Its a federal crime to make false statements on a loan or credit application, to misrepresent your Social Security Number, and to obtain an Employer Identification Number from the Internal Revenue Service under false pretenses.

Thanks to the new Telemarketing Sales Rule, it's also a crime for telemarketers who offer credit repair services to require you to pay until six months after they've delivered the services.

What to do if you've had Problems with Credit Repair Agencies:

Many states have laws strictly regulating credit repair companies. States may be helpful if you've lost money to credit repair scams.

If you've had a problem with a credit repair company, dot be embarrassed to report the company. Contact your local consumer affairs office or your state attorney general (AG). Many AGs have toll-free consumer hotlines. Check with your local directory assistance.

You also may wish to contact the FTC. Although the Commission cannot resolve individual credit problems for consumers, it can act against a company if it sees a pattern of possible law violations. If you believe a company has engaged in credit fraud, send your complaints to: Correspondence Branch, Federal Trade Commission, Washington, DC 20580.

The National Fraud Information Center (NFIC) also accepts consumer complaints. You can reach NFIC at 1-800-876-7060,

9 a.m. - 5:30 p.m. EST, Monday - Friday, or at http://www.fraud.org on the Internet. NFIC is a private, nonprofit organization that operates a consumer assistance phone line to provide services and help in filing complaints. NFIC also forwards appropriate complaints to the FTC for entry on its telemarketing fraud database.

Back to "Credit Repair Kit"

APPENDIX 5

BANK RATE MONITOR™

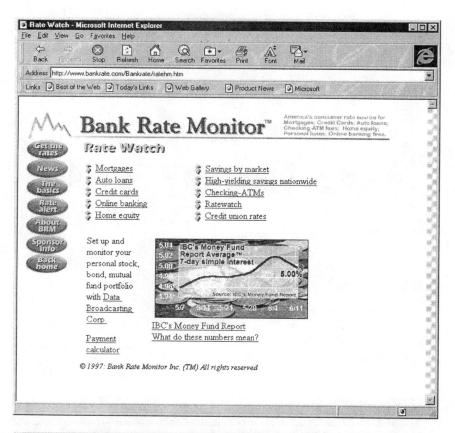

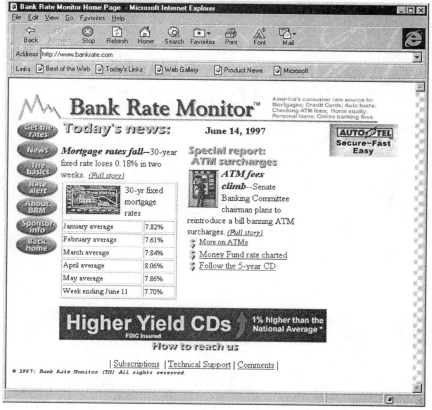

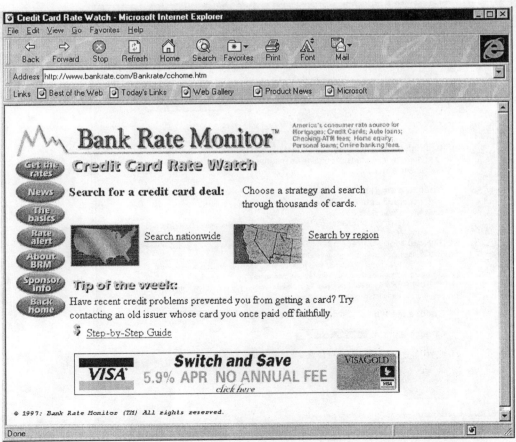

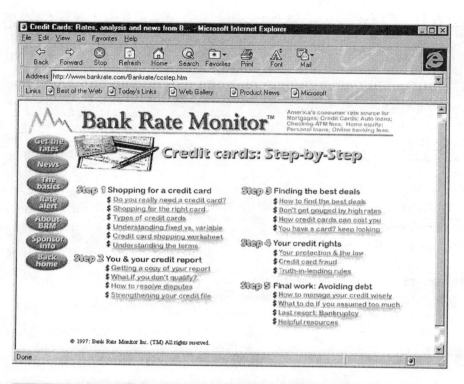

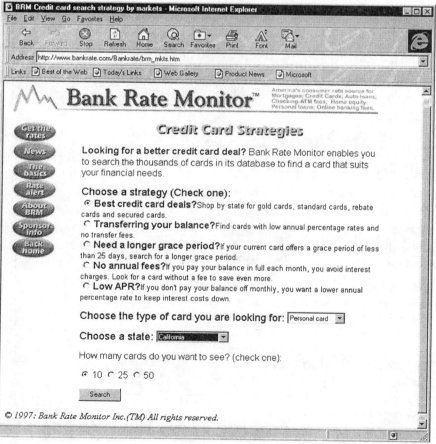

E-MAIL CARD FRAUD? INVESTIGATORS CHECKING PRE-APPROVED OFFERS

N. PALM BEACH, Florida — The Nevada Financial Institutions Division is investigating Consumer Money Markets, Inc., a Henderson, Nevada company that is e-mailing, via the Internet, preapproved credit card solicitations. At least one offers a 17.99% rate.

"We have received information from the Connecticut Department of Banking relative to what appears to be at least an unlicensed credit card solicitation from Nevada over the Internet," says Burns Baker, Nevada Financial Institutions Division Deputy Commissioner. "Apparently, they want a $149.95 up-front fee, and they represent that anyone who sends in a fee and becomes a member will have at no additional cost an unsecured Visa or MasterCard processed. This money card they're soliciting is nothing more than an in-house credit card to buy merchandise."

"Dear Future Cardholder," says one solicitation by the same company with the same phone number. "Congratulations! You have been approved for a $2,000 unsecured credit line," the e-mail, offering a "MoneyFirstCard" begins. The credit limit is $2,000. "Bank affiliation: NONE," is the only clue that the credit card is not from a bank.

ONLY WORKS FOR CATALOG SALES

Baker said that a copy of the solicitation he had, also by a company called "CMM" at the same phone number, promotes a "MoneyCard" by Ocean Independent Bank.

"If we were aware of an address, we would issue them a cease and desist order," Baker declared. Actually, says Paul Welch, manager of the financial division of Consumer Money Markets, Inc., reached by phone, the preapproved credit line is being offered not through a bank. It is only good for purchases from the company's 100-page catalog, which, he says, contains more than 400 items, including gifts, tools, camping equipment, electronics and silver. The company will also issue its cardholders cash advances on the card at a fee of $5 or 10% of the cash advance, whichever is greater.

To obtain a cash advance, a customer provides checking or savings account information, and within 72 hours, the company says it will deposit funds into the customer's checking or savings account.

To obtain the unsecured card, Welch says, customers must pay a one-time $149.95 membership fee, but they get a $100 discount for the first credit purchase over $200 with the card. The card also offers an optional service for $29.95, which increases the credit line up to 150% after the first credit purchase or cash advance and defer the balance for 90 days if the cardholder becomes involuntarily unemployed or disabled.

FEE REQUESTED

Customers sign up for its card through electronic draft of a checking account, by a Federal Express pick-up of a check or money order, or by having it billed to a credit card they already have, Welch said. For an added $19.95 fee, the company promises to rush processing and get the package to the cardholder two weeks sooner.

The company also says it works with a "network of banks" to get cardholders a Visa or MasterCard, but Welch initially declined to provide more information on the bank network.

In the early 1990s, the Federal Trade Commission came down on at least two companies that it claimed deceptively sold "gold cards," which were not Visa or MasterCard, but credit cards useable only for the companies' own catalogs. Nevada Financial Institutions Division Commissioner Scott Walshaw notes there were a number of such operations. "Somebody applies for it and it turns out the gold card can be used to buy their merchandise at inflated prices," he reflected.

If Consumer Money Markets, Inc.'s offer sounds slightly similar, there are major differences, according to CMM's Welch. Among them, he said: The merchandise in the CMM catalog is at competitive prices. "We have no computers in the catalog. We can't compete with companies like Best Buy."

The Better Business Bureau lists Jimmy A. Miller as president of Consumer Money Markets, Inc., and claimed that although the company has applied for membership, the BBB can't approve businesses in business six months or less. "We've been in operation since September 1996," Welch said.

PROCESS FAIR, COMPANY SAYS

Welch likens his company to the American Fair Credit Association, a marketing company that says it arranges for members, typically with poor credit, to obtain an unsecured credit card. But they pay a monthly membership fee for a host of services.

American Fair Credit Association, however, is promoted by 360 AFCA "agents" who drop take-one boxes at area businesses. The agents, in return, get a commission of 30% to 40% of the first year's dues.

But Consumer Money Markets, Inc., Welch says, has no such network of agents.

"I can't confirm or deny we're looking at a specific company or practice," said Lucy Morris, assistant director of credit practices of the Federal Trade Commission, when queried about the company.

"The commission has done at least 15 cases already dealing with fraud on the Internet," Morris said. "We've done several fraud cases concerning representations on the Internet—credit repair fraud and business opportunity scams. We're monitoring companies under our jurisdiction for compliance for statutes we enforce.

Morris noted the FTC recently settled with five auto manufacturers for their lease and credit advertisements. "You can't advertise that you can get a car for zero down when there are least inception fees that are not disclosed except in hidden, fine print."

She also said the FTC, upon surfing the Internet, found some 500 advertisements that looked like deceptive pyramid schemes and notified all those people.

"If they're fraudulent outside of cyberspace, they're fraudulent inside cyberspace," Morris warned.

15 USC Sec. 1681i (01/24/94)

§ 1681i. Procedure in case of disputed accuracy

(a) Dispute; reinvestigation

If the completeness or accuracy of any item of information contained in his file is disputed by a consumer, and such dispute is directly conveyed to the consumer reporting agency by the consumer, the consumer reporting agency shall within a reasonable period of time reinvestigate and record the current status of that information unless it has reasonable grounds to believe that the dispute by the consumer is frivolous or irrelevant. If after such reinvestigation such information is found to be inaccurate or can no longer be verified, the consumer reporting agency shall promptly delete such information. The presence of contradictory information in the consumer's file does not in and of itself constitute reasonable grounds for believing the dispute is frivolous or irrelevant.

• (b) Statement of dispute

If the reinvestigation does not resolve the dispute, the consumer may file a brief statement setting forth the nature of the dispute. The consumer reporting agency may limit such statements to not more than one hundred words if it provides the consumer with assistance in writing a clear summary of the dispute.

• (c) Notification of consumer dispute in subsequent consumer reports

Whenever a statement of a dispute is filed, unless there is reasonable grounds to believe that it is frivolous or irrelevant, the consumer reporting agency shall, in any subsequent consumer report containing the information in question, clearly note that it is disputed by the consumer and provide either the consumer's statement or a clear and accurate codification or summary thereof.

• (d) Notification of deletion of disputed information

Following any deletion of information which is found to be inaccurate or whose accuracy can no longer be verified or any notation as to disputed information, the consumer reporting agency shall, at the request of the consumer, furnish notification that the item has been deleted or the statement, codification or summary pursuant to subsection (b) or (c) of this section to any person specifically designated by the consumer who has within two years prior thereto received a consumer report for employment purposes, or within six months prior thereto received a consumer report for any other purpose, which contained the deleted or disputed information. The consumer reporting agency shall clearly and conspicuously disclose to the consumer his rights to make such a request Such disclosure shall be made at or prior to the time the information is deleted or the consumer's statement regarding the disputed information is received.

15 USC Sec. 1681j (01/24/94)

<u>UNITED STATES CODE</u>
<u>TITLE 15</u>- COMMERCE AND TRADE
<u>CHAPTER 41</u>- CONSUMER CREDIT PROTECTION
SUBCHAPTER III - CREDIT REPORTING AGENCIES

§ 1681j. Charges for disclosures

A consumer reporting agency shall make all disclosures pursuant to section <u>1681g</u> of this title and furnish all consumer reports pursuant to section 1681i(d) of this title without charge to the consumer if; within thirty days after receipt by such consumer of a notification pursuant to section <u>1681m</u> of this title or notification from a debt collection agency affiliated with such consumer reporting agency stating that the consumer's credit rating may be or has been adversely affected, the consumer makes a request under section <u>1681g</u> or 1681i(d) of this title. Otherwise, the consumer reporting agency may impose a reasonable charge on the consumer for making disclosure to such consumer pursuant to section 1<u>681g</u> of this title, the charge for which shall be indicated to the consumer prior to making disclosure; and for furnishing notifications, statements, summaries, or codifications to person designated by the consumer pursuant to section 1681i(d) of this title, the charge for which shall be indicated to the consumer prior to furnishing such information and shall not exceed the charge that the consumer reporting agency would impose on each designated recipient for a consumer report except that no charge may be made for notifying such persons of the deletion of information which is found to be inaccurate or which can no longer be verified.

Home page | Mortgages | Savings | Home Equity | Credit Cards | Consumer Loans | Banking Tips | Banking News | BRM Publications | Register]

How to use your secured credit card list... Below, you'll see a condensed list of secured card issuers. You'll see their card interest rate, application fee, annual fee, their minimum and maximum line of credit, the amount of deposit they require, and a code letter (e.g., "a" or "b") that describes their restrictions. To read the actual restrictions, look at the end of the list. Also note, below, the income requirements for their secured cards.

Coming Soon...
More free and timely information on credit cards, whether issued by your local bank or a bank across the country. You'll know the terms, rates, fees and billing cycles...stay tuned.

Secured credit card issuers

Institution / Location /Phone	Rate on purchases/ Grace period	Application Annual fee	Min. /Max. Line	Deposit Required	Restrictions
American Pacific Bank, Aumsville,OR (800)610-1201	17.40%/30 days-billing	None/$25	$400/$15,000	$400 to $15,000	a,b,c,h,j, k,m,n,t,u,$
Bank of Hoven, South Dakota (800)777-7735	19.80%/25 days-billing	None/$39	$300/$5,000	$300/$5,000	b,c,n,$
Bank One Tempe, AZ (800)544-4110	21.20%V/25 days-billing	None/$25	$500/$5,000	$500 to $5,000	a,b,c,k,p,v
Chase Manhattan Bank USA Wilmington, DE (800)482-4273	17.90%/30 days-billing	None/$20	$300/$5,000	$300 to $5,000	b
Citibank, Sioux Falls, SD (800)743-1332	17.65%V/20 days-billing	None/$20	$300/$5,000	$300 to $5,000	a,c,$
Citizens Bank Riverside, R.I. (800)438-9222	15.65%/25 days-billing	None/$25	$300/$10,000	$300 to $10,000	b,c,i,$
Community Bank of Parker, CO (800)779-8472	15.90%/25 days-billing	None/$29	$300/$5,000	$500 to $5,000	a,b,d,e,g,j,k, l,m,n,o,r,s,u,$
Cross Country Bank, New Castle, DE (302) 322-3210	20.99%V/0 days-posting	$39/$39	$300/$5,000	$200 to $5,000	a,b,c,k,$
Federal Savings Bank Rogers, AR (800)290-9060	9.72%V/25 days-posting	None/$39	$250/$10,000	$250 to $10,000	b,c,g,k,$
First Consumers National Bank Beaverton, OR (800)937-3795	18.90%V/30 days-billing	None/$39	$100/100%, 150% or 200% of deposit[w]	$100 min.	a,b,c,k,l, p,u,w,$
First National Bank of Brookings, SD (800)658-3660	18.90/25 days-billing	None/$35	$250/$5,000	$250 to $5,000	a,b,k,$
First National Bank of Marin, San Rafael, CA (702)269-1200	18.84%/25 days-billing	$60/$35	$200/$2,500	$200 to $2,500	b,c,j
First Premier Bank Sioux Falls, SD (800)987-5521	18.90%/25 days-billing	None/$45	$400/$10,000	$400 to $10,000	a,b,c,k,n

Household Bank Salinas, CA (800)477-6000	20.65%V/25 days-billing	None/$25	$300/$10,000	$300 to $10,000	a,c,i,n
Key Bank & Trust, Havre de Grace, MD (800)539-5398	19.40%/25 days-posting	None/$35	$525/$3,000	$350 to $2000	a,b,c,g,k,l,$
Marine Midland Bank Buffalo, NY (800) 850-3144	21.90%/25 days-posting	None/$25	$300/$5,000	$300 to $5,000	a,b,c,f
Orchard Bank Ontario, OR (800)873-7307	15.50%V/30 days-billing 18.90%V/30 days-billing	None/$45 None/$35	$200/$15,000 $200/$15,000	$200/$15,000 $200/$15,000	a,h,k,n,$ a,h,k,n,$
Peoples Bank Bridgeport, CT (800) 262-4442	16.90%/25 days-billing	None/$25	$500-$1,000 - $1,500	$500-$1,000 - $1,500	b,c,e,f
Sanwa Bank San Francisco (800)237-2692	15.90%/25 days-billing	$25/$35	$500/$5,000	$625 to $5,750	b,c,i,n,q,s,t
Sterling Bank & Trust Southfield, MI (800) 603-0600	22.00%/25 days-posting	$49/$78	$200/$5,000	$200 to $5,200	a,b,c,n,t
United Bank of Philadelphia (800) 255-3807	17.99%/0 days-posting	None/$35	$300/$5,000	$200 to $5,000	a,b,c,k,n,$

EXPLANATION OF RESTRICTIONS:

a -must be U.S. citizen; permanent resident; **b** -must have Social Security number; or taxpayer ID; **c** -must be 18 years old; **d** -must be 21; **e** -employed one year; **f** -no prior credit problems; **g** -no delinquencies in past six months; **h** -Chapter 13 bankruptcy must be six months old; or over one year old; **i** -no bankruptcy on credit record; **j** -no bankruptcy in past six months; **k** -bankruptcy discharged; **l** -no excessive credit card debt or Federal tax liens; **m** -not available in Maine; **n** -not available in Wisconsin; **o** -not available in Illinois; **p** -North Carolina; **q** -Florida; **r** -Michigan; **s** -Iowa; **t** -Puerto Rico; **u** -Vermont; **v** -Massachusetts; **w** -$2,500 max. unsecured portion, **V**-variable rate.

$-Income requirements: $165 weekly (Key Bank & Trust), $700 monthly (First National Bank of Brookings), $1000 monthly (Citizens Bank), $1,200 monthly (Community Bank of Parker), $5,000 annual (Bank of Hoven), $8,000 annual (Citibank), $9,600 annual (Federal Savings Bank), $10,000 annual (American Pacific Bank, Cross Country Bank, Orchard Bank, United Bank of Philadelphia), $12,000 annual (First Consumers National Bank).

APPENDIX 6

SAMPLE LETTERS OF DISPUTE

DISPUTE LETTER ONE

Date

Your full name
Your birthdate
Your social security no.
Your full address

Dear sir:

The following entries on my credit report are inaccurate and do not belong to me:

Entry one: {account name and number}_____
Entry two: {account name and number}_____

Please investigate these entries and remove them as soon as possible. Please send me a corrected copy of my credit report.

Thank you,

Signature

DISPUTE LETTER TWO

Date

Your full name
Your birthdate
Your social security no.
Your full address

Dear sir:

Three weeks ago I sent you a letter requesting that certain inaccurate information be removed from my credit report. To date I have had no response from you. Enclosed is a copy of that letter. Please remove these items at once and send me a corrected copy of my report, as you are required to do under the Fair Credit Reporting Act. If you do not comply with the law I will file a complaint with the Federal Trade Commission.

Thank you,

Signature

Enclosure

DISPUTE LETTER THREE

Date

Your full name
Your birthdate
Your social security no.
Your full address

Dear sir:

Two weeks ago I sent you a second letter regarding inaccurate information in my credit report. Enclosed is a copy of that letter. Three weeks prior to the second letter I sent you original communication regarding this matter. A copy of that letter is also enclosed.

The "reasonable time" provisions of the Fair Credit Reporting Act have elapsed and I formally demand that these items be removed. I will be filing a complaint with the Federal Trade Commission over your behavior in this matter.

If I do not receive a corrected copy of my credit report with the inaccurate accounts removed within ten days, I will take legal action against you.

Thank you,

Signature

Enclosures

FEDERAL TRADE COMMISSION COMPLAINT LETTER

Date

Your name
Your address
Your telephone number

Dear sirs:

I have been attempting to remove inaccurate information with the
_____ credit bureau under the Fair Credit Reporting Act.
The bureau has refused to comply with its obligations under the law.
Enclosed are copies of my correspondence with the bureau. I would
appreciate any help you could provide in this matter.

Thank you,

Signature

CREDITOR PAYOFF DEAL LETTER

Date

Your name
Your address

Dear {name of credit manager}:

In reference to our telephone discussion of the following account, this is the agreement to cease reporting this account to the credit bureau in exchange for the following payment arrangement.

{add if account sent to collection agency}:
You also agree to have **{name of collection agency}**, to which my account was referred by you, remove their entry from my credit report in exchange for the following payment arrangement:

I, **{your name}**, agree to pay **{amount of payment}**, in **{number of installments}**, on account **{account number}**, in exchange for this account no longer being reported to the credit bureau and the collection agency entry removed from my credit report.

Your Name   Credit Manager Name

Your Signature   His Signature and Date

Upon receipt of this signed agreement I will forward payment.

APPENDIX 7

DTEC OVERVIEW

(EQUIFAX)

DTEC OVERVIEW

A. DESCRIPTION:

DTEC allows customers to search the entire database by entering only the nine (9) digit Social Security Number of the subject to obtain identification information. It helps customers locate individuals who have not provided their names accurately, or whose addresses are no longer, or have never been, valid.

In April 1991, two (2) output variations of DTEC were introduced. The two (2) versions are to differentiate between "consumer" and "non-consumer" opportunities. In some instances, a customer may receive the complete DTEC output; in other instances, the customer may receive **ONLY** the name and address.

Listed below are situations under which DTEC may be sold:

1. **"Consumer Purposes (Complete DTEC Information Available):**

   - Credit granting.
   - Collection of money owed via a credit transaction.
   - Employment purposes.
   - Obtaining a license.
   - Location of beneficiaries (insurance, stockholders, pension funds, unclaimed assets or property).
   - Child Support payment enforcement.
   - Opening/reviewing checking/savings accounts.
   - Verification of a credit file "No Record".
   - Location of stockholder or pensioner.
   - Default on loans.
   - Location of former employee (send W-2, retirement benefits).

2. **"Non-Consumer Purposes (Name & Address Information ONLY):**

   - Claims/Subrogation.
   - Process servers to locate witnesses or defendants.
   - Government agencies who lack a "permissible" purpose.
   - College/University alumni associations.
   - Mail returns.
   - Law enforcement
   - Location of relatives listed on a credit application to obtain information on how to locate a debtor.

3. **Corporate decisions have been made <u>not to consider offering</u> DTEC in the following situations:**

- Bail Bondsmen.
- Genealogical or Heir researchers or locators.
- Detective Agencies or private investigative agencies.
  To locate for repossession of property, where the property is held by someone other than the debtor.
- To locate missing children.

4. **The DTEC product manager <u>MUST</u> be consulted, <u>PRIOR TO PROVIDING THE SERVICE</u>, if a customer requests DTEC for situations other than those stated above. This is a broad summary of various bases and the FCRA. In each case, the details of applicable bases, policies and the section of the FCRA must be consulted and complied with.**

B. INPUT:

Use your normal procedure to sign-on. After "PROCEED" message appears, enter:

DTEC – 098-76-5432 (Social Security Number).

NOTE: DTEC <u>cannot</u> be accessed with "E", "EF", or "Q" sign-ons.

C. OUTPUT:

Posting of inquiries – "DTEC" inquiry is posted to the file; purge in six (6) months. When the complete DTEC information is delivered, the inquiry is viewable for consumer disclosure only.

The output will be up to four (4) multiple files or a "NO RECORD" message. DTEC searches the entire database for a 9-for- social security match. There are three DTEC social security warnings: never issued; deceased; misused.

- "Consumer" DTEC Output:

- Public Utilities

D. COMMON OBJECTIONS AND ANSWERS

1. Objection: If I cannot access the credit report, what good will DTEC be to me?

   Answer: DTEC allows you to search the entire ECIS national database by entering only the Social Security Number to determine identifying information on a person. It helps locate consumers who have not provided their names accurately or whose addresses have changed.

2. Objection: Why do different names appear for one Social Security Number? Is there something wrong with your system?

   Answer: There are several reasons why different names may be returned for one Social Security Number:

- An AKA (Also Known As) name is being used.
- The digits in the Social Security Number for one of the names listed have been erroneously transposed.
- A person is using his/her spouse's (or other relative's) Social Security Number in error. Each person is assigned a unique Social Security Number. The Social Security Administration has never instructed persons to consider a relative's Social Security Number as their own.
- Attempted or actual fraud has been perpetrated.

E. FEATURES

FEATURE	BENEFIT	EVIDENCE (PROOF)
• **Easy to Use**	Saves time and money—enter only Social Security Number.	Demonstration
• **Nationwide, systemwide search**	Saves time by locating multiple files when names and/or addresses are incorrect.	Demonstration
	Locates files previously not found	Demonstration
	Locates files when current address is unknown.	Demonstration
	Provides information even if false information is given.	Warning messages
• **DTEC warning messages**	Provides protection from attempted fraud or input errors.	Warning messages
• **Locate System**	Provides more information, less expensively than a hit or miss internal system.	Demonstration
	Professional, up-to-date information provided quickly.	Demonstration

DTEC-098-76-5432

****
SOCIAL SECURITY NUMBER REPORTED MISUSED.
****

M1 OF 4 NM-BEAR, YOGI...CA-1801, BOO BOO, LN, ATLANTA, GA, 5/90
   FA-1321, N. JOHNSON, ST., NEW YORK, NY., 11/89 ES-DRAFTSMAN, PARTRIDGE
     SS-098-76-5432 AGE 44
M2 OF 4 NM-MONSTER, GINGER CA-666, SESAME, ST, ATLANTA, GA 30303, 11/87
     SS-098-76-5432
M3 OF 4 NM-MOUSE, MINNIE CA-123, MAIN, ST, ATLANTA, GA 30303, 08/87
   FA-123, MAIN, ST, SANTA ROSA, CA 95401, 10/86 ES-MOUSE, DISNEY
     SS-098-76-5432 AGE 34
M4 OF 4 NM-STARR, BRENDA, A CA-444, MAIN, ST, ATLANTA, GA, 01/86
   FA-BOX 44, PO, ATLANTA, GA, 01/86 ES-, REPORTER
     SS-098-76-5432&

END OF REPORT   EQUIFAX AND AFFILIATES   12/13/91

"Non-Consumer" DTEC Output:

DTEC-098-76-5432

****
SOCIAL SECURITY NUMBER REPORTED MISUSED.
****

M1 OF 4 NM-BEAR, YOGI...CA-1801, BOO BOO, LN, ATLANTA, GA, 5/90
   FA-1321, N. JOHNSON, ST., NEW YORK, NY., 11/89
M2 OF 4 NM-MONSTER, GINGER CA-666, SESAME, ST, ATLANTA, GA 30303, 11/87
M3 OF 4 NM-MOUSE, MINNIE CA-123, MAIN, ST, ATLANTA, GA 30303, 08/87
   FA-123, MAIN, ST, SANTA ROSA, CA 95401, 10/86
M4 OF 4 NM-STARR, BRENDA, A CA-444, MAIN, ST, ATLANTA, GA, 01/86
   FA-BOX 44, PO, ATLANTA, GA, 01/86

END OF REPORT   EQUIFAX AND AFFILIATES   12/13/91

If there is a "NO RECORD", the following message is received:

---

51 NO RECORD FOUND &

END OF REPORT   EQUIFAX AND AFFILIATES   12/13/91

DTEC SOCIAL SECURITY WARNING MESSAGES:

- SOCIAL SECURITY NUMBER HAS NEVER BEEN ISSUED BY SOCIAL SECURITY ADMINISTRATION

- SOCIAL SECURITY NUMBER IS ISSUED TO A PERSON REPORTED WHO HAS BEEN DECEASED

- SOCIAL SECURITY NUMBER HAS BEEN REPORTED MISUSED

ACCESS METHODS

- DAT
- PC
- Tape to Tape
- System-To-System

PROSPECTS

- College/University Alumni Associations
- Corporate Transfer Agents/Stockholder Administrators
- Financial Institutions
- Government Agencies
- Hospitals
- Insurance Companies
- Law Enforcement
- Pension Fund Administrators
- Petroleum Industry

FEATURES	BENEFITS
Firm Name	Inquiries from other collection agencies or members with trade lines can tell a collector how urgent the situation is and help them prioritize their collection efforts.
Date of Inquiry	Saves time – collector can call the credit grantors with the most recent contact with the debtor.
Sectioned Report (ID, Trade, Inquiry)	Saves time – easy-to-read format.
SAFESCAN	Saves time – identified potential fraud. The collector will not waste time attempting to collect on the account.

APPENDIX 8

ID REPORT AND FINDERS OVERVIEWS

(EQUIFAX)

ID REPORT OVERVIEW

A. DESCRIPTION:

Based on the standard search process, the ID Report contains only identification information.

In April 1991, two (2) output variations of the I.D. Report were introduced. The two (2) versions are to distinguish between "consumer" and "non-consumer" opportunities. In some instances, a customer may receive the complete I.D. Report output; in other instance, the customer may receive **ONLY** the name, addresses and AKA's/former names.

Listed below are situations where I.D. Report may be sold:

1. **"Consumer Purposes (Complete I.D. Report Information Available)**

   - Credit granting.
   - Collection of money owed via a credit transaction.
   - Employment purposes.
   - Obtaining a license.
   - Location of beneficiaries (insurance, stockholders, pension funds, unclaimed assets or property).
   - Child support payment enforcement.
   - Opening/reviewing checking/savings accounts.
   - Verification of a credit file "No Record".
   - Location of stockholder or pensioner.
   - Default on loans.
   - Location of former employee (send W-2, retirement benefits).

2. **"Non-Consumer" Purposes (Name, address and AKA Information ONLY):**

   - Claims/Subrogation.
   - Process servers to locate witnesses or defendants.
   - Government agencies who lack a "permissible" purpose.
   - College/University alumni associations.
   - Mail returns.
   - Law enforcement.
   - Location of relatives listed on a credit application to obtain information on how to locate a debtor.

3. Corporate decisions have been made not to consider offering I.D. Report in the following situations
   - Bail Bondsmen.
   - Genealogical or Heir researchers or locators.
   - Detective Agencies or private investigative agencies.
   - To locate for repossession of property, where the property is held by someone other than the debtor.
   - To locate missing children.

4. The I.D. Report Product Manager **MUST** be consulted, **PRIOR TO PROVIDING THE** SERVICE, if a customer requests I.D. Report for situations other than those stated above. This is a broad summary of various bases and the Fair Credit Reporting Act (FCRA). In each case, the details of applicable bases, policies and the section of the FCRA must be consulted and compiled with.

B. INPUT:

Member signs on in the normal manner using the report indicator "I".

Example: 999AA12345-XX,Mary,I.

C. OUTPUT:

Posting of inquiries – "ID" inquiry is posted to the file; purged in six (6) months. When the complete I.D. Report information is delivered, the inquiry is viewable for consumer disclosure only.

---

1. "CONSUMER" I.D. REPORT OUTPUT:

"001 EQUIFAX CREDIT INFORMATION SERVICES 5505 P TREE DUNWOODY RD NE, STE 600, PO BOX 740241, ATLANTA, GA 30374-0241, 800-685-1111

"EEWING, JOHN., SR. SINCE 08/19/91 FAD 12/12/91   FN-288
123, SOUTHFORK, DR. OZ, GA 000999, DAT RPTD 06/91
456, JUPITER RD, DALLAS, GA 30132, DAT RPTD 11/91
BDS-06/21/40,SSS-666-55-4444
01 ES-,QQQQ
02 EF-,EWING OIL
03 E2-,ANYTOWN INC.

End of Equifax Identification Information Report–12/13/91   SAFESCAN

2. "NON-CONSUMER" I.D. REPORT OUTPUT:

"001 EQUIFAX CREDIT INFORMATION SERVICES 5505 P TREE DUNWOODY RD NE, STE 600 PO BOX 740241, ATLANTA, GA 30374-0241, 800-685-1111

"EEWING, JOHN., SR. SINCE 08/19/91 FAD 12/12/91   FN-288
123, SOUTHFORK, DR. OZ, GA 000999, DAT RPTD 06/91
456, JUPITER RD, DALLAS, GA 30132, DAT RPTD 11/91

End of Equifax Identification Information Report–12/13/91   SAFESCAN

3. "If there is a "No Record", the following is received:

"001 EQUIFAX CREDIT INFORMATION SERVICES 5505 P TREE DUNWOODY RD NE, STE 600 PO BOX 740241, ATLANTA, GA 30374-0241, 800-685-1111
51 NO RECORD FOUND-CHECK INPUT, USE SS# AND ZIP CODE IF AVAILABLE.

End of Equifax Identification Information Report–12/13/91   SAFESCAN

D. ACCESS METHODS:

- CRT
- DAT
- PC
- TAPE-TO-TAPE

E. PROSPECTS:

- College/University Alumni Associations
- Corporate Transfer Agents/Stockholder Administrators
- Financial Institutions
- Government Agencies
- Hospitals
- Insurance Companies
- Law Enforcement
- Pension Fund Administrators
- Petroleum Industry

F. COMMON OBJECTIONS & ANSWERS:

Why should I use the I.D. Report?

- If you have a permissible purpose to obtain this information as defined by the FCRA, the I.D. Report can return identification information, including the Social Security Number. By using the SSN with DTEC, you can determine whether other identities have been used with that SSN.

When you have only the name and address and are attempting to locate a person, the I.D. Report can provide current and former addresses.

G. FEATURES/BENEFITS:

FEATURES	**BENEFITS**
• Easy to Use	Saves time.
• Nationwide, systemwide search	Saves time by locating multiple files.
• Available with SAFESCAN	Provides protection from attempted fraud.

FINDERS OVERVIEW

A. DESCRIPTION:

FINDERS was developed by and for the collection industry. We asked them what type of product they would like to see available for the Collection industry to assist in skiptracing; the result is FINDERS.

FINDERS consists of the parts of the credit report that are most valuable to collectors who are trying to locate debtors for whom they do not have a valid address or telephone number (also called "skips" by the industry).

B. INPUT:

Sign on in the normal manner. The FINDERS report indicator is "G".

Example:
999AA12345-XX,DLS,G.

C. OUTPUT:

FINDERS inquiries will display on Acrofile and Acrofile Plus.

See next page for example.

D. ACCESS METHODS:

- DAT
- PC
- SYSTEM-TO-SYSTEM

E. PROSPECTS:

- In-House Collection Departments
- Third Party Collection Agencies

F. COMMON OBJECTIONS AND ANSWERS:

1. OBJECTION: FINDERS costs too much.

   ANSWER: When you consider the information FINDERS provides and the price compared to other skip locate products, don't you agree FINDERS is a good value?

2. OBJECTION: My collectors have been using another product for quite a while. It will take them time to learn to use FINDERS.

    ANSWER: Equifax will provide training for your associates. Since FINDERS has an easy-to-read format and only contains the information that is most helpful to your collectors, they should become comfortable with FINDERS very quickly.

3. OBJECTION: I need account status and delinquency information.

    ANSWER: I understand there are times when you need account status and delinquency information. ACROFILE and ACROFILE PLUS, Equifax's full credit reports, will provide this information and also account balances, public records and collection items.

4. OBJECTION: I'm getting good results from the product I'm currently using.

    ANSWER: You'll get better results with FINDERS. Compare FINDERS with the product you are using. Take a random sample of skipped accounts. Pull FINDERS and the product you are currently using on each account. Evaluate each account to decide which product provides the most information. FINDERS will help you locate more debtors, particularly debtors with post office box and rural route addresses (most other products cannot locate debtors with these addresses).

G. FEATURES/BENEFITS:

FEATURES	BENEFITS
Subject's full name	Verifies identity, may provide a previously known middle initial or suffix that, with additional research, may locate the debtor.
Spouse's full name	Can pull spouse's file—may find additional information. May include spouse if suit is filed.
Identifies AKA's	May find information under different names.
Addresses and previous addresses	May identify a new address. Identifies previous addresses. Collector can locate and call neighbors who may have information.
P.O. and rural route addresses	Can find addresses most other locate products are not able to find.
SSN	Can be used with DTEC to locate a debtor.
Employment	Collectors need to know before filing suit to garnish wages. May reach the debtor at work or may get information from the debtor's current and previous work associates.
Date address reported	The date the address was put on the file.
Bankruptcy "Warning" message	Indicates bankruptcy information on the full credit file. These accounts can be prioritized.
Trade Line	May locate a debtor through information they receive from another creditor.

Account Number	Saves time – creditor being called can locate their customer's account quickly.
Date Reported	Provides date Equifax received the information
Member Number	Provides identifying information when contacting a creditor.
Account Type (I,O,R)	Identifies type of credit being used. An "R" from a bank usually indicates a Visa or MasterCard. When the collector locates the person he/she can suggest the debtor request a cash advance to pay the debt.
Telephone Number	Saves time and money – no need to look up the member's telephone number or pay costly directory assistance charges.
Availability of Telephone Contacts	More information – most telephone numbers listed in the Trade Line section can be reached between 8:00 a.m. and 5:00 p.m.
Date of Last Activity (DLA)	Saves time – by calling the creditor where the activity has been most recent.
Inquiry	Can call other members with recent inquiries. They may have a current address, telephone number or employment from a recent application.

OUTPUT:

EQUIFAX CREDIT ATLANTA 3 EXECUTIVE PARK DR
PO BOX 95007, ATLANTA, GA 30347
JOHNSON, PERCY, A.DIANA SINCE 10/11/82 FAD 10/31/91
1600, PEACHTREE, ST, ATLANTA 30369, CRT RPTD 10/89
123 HARBOR CT, MIAMI, FL, CRT RPTD 01/84
555, COWBOY DR, DALLAS, OR 97303, CRT RPTD 12/82
AKA-LUCUS, JOHN
BDS-12/22/50,SSN-111-22-3333, SEX-M,MAR-M,DEP-2

ES-ENGR,LOCKHEED,ATLANTA,GA, EMP 09/89, VER 11/89,$3000
EF-ENGR,FLORIDA POWER,MIAMI,FL,10/84,VER01/85,$2000
E2-TEACHER,DALLAS COMMUNITY COLL,DALLAS,OR,EMP 10/82,VER5/83,$1800
 ****WARNING****BANKRUPTCY ON FILE,FULL CREDIT REPORT IS ADVISED

TRADE LINE INFORMATION

Acct Number	Date Rptd	Member No	Firm Name	Type	Telephone No	Last Acv
123456789012345678	10/91	404BB45678	CRESENT	R	(404)555-5555	7/91
8888888888	08/91	404BB56846	MACYS	R	(404)123-4567	06/90
987654321	06/91	404DC78697	FSB UTAH	O	(404)456-7777	05/91
	03/91	404BB7684	ENCY BRIT	I	(312)789-8899	01/91
1357997531	11/90	404BB991	F&M NATLBK	I	(404)922-0001	09/90

INQUIRY INFORMATION

Member Number	Firm Name	Telephone Number	Date of Inquiry
404DC12125	RICHS	(404)449-1234	09/13/91
404FA8765	GMAC	(404)722-8090	09/09/91
404ZZ52446	SYS PL&SUP	(218)444-4444	08/08/91
404FA15551	FORD FIN	(404)723-9876	06/24/91

End of Equifax Identification Information Report–12/13/91   SAFESCAN

- ID SECTION

  - Contains all the ID information found in the ACROFILE OR ACROFILE PLUS.
  - Bankruptcy "warning" message.

- TRADE SECTION

  - Accounts with activity reported in the past 24 months in descending order.
  - Account Number
  - Date Reported
  - Member Number
  - Plain language firm/member name
  - Type of Account (I,O,R)
  - Telephone number of firm/member
  - Date of the inquiry.

INQUIRY SECTION

  - Inquiries within the past 12 months, in descending order.
  - Member Number
  - Plain language firm/member name
  - Telephone number of firm/member
  - Date of the inquiry

APPENDIX 9

CREDIT CARD TIPS

CREDIT CARD TIPS from.....

http://financiallywired.com/financiallywired/credit_card/tips.html

Rolling, rolling, rolling down the river...To help you, Sage Financial has compiled a database of Credit Card tips, which you will find updated on a regular basis. This will be the one source for answers to your credit card questions. So let's charge ahead and discover what's in Store for now.

1. Call one of the major credit bureaus to obtain a copy of your current credit report. Credit report information can significantly impact your ability to obtain credit on favorable terms. Two of the major credit bureaus are:

- TRW Information Services- (800)632-7654
- Equifax Credit Information Services- (800) 685-1111

Sage Advice: Credit bureaus are required by Federal law to allow you to see a copy of your report but they are not obligated to provide you with a copy unless your state law requires it. As a matter of customer service, most credit bureaus will provide you a copy for a fee.

2. If you have a problem with your credit report, note the errors, and return it to them with an explanation.

Sage Advice: If the bureau can't prove you wrong within twenty-five days, they must remove the disputed information from your report.

3. The credit bureau will provide other major services to you for a fee. Examples include increased access to your credit report, or an analysis of your financial standing.

Sage Advice: These additional services are probably unnecessary for most people, unless you have a troubled credit history or potential complexities such as a junior, common name, or have been a past victim of fraud.

4. Maintain good credit at all times so that you can continue to take advantage of one of the main benefits of credit cards: convenience.

Sage Advice: Credit Cards protect you from substantial financial loss by reducing the amount of cash you need to have on hand at any time and providing a ready access toll-free phone number if you card is stolen/lost.

5. Not all Visa and MasterCards are the same. The terms and features of a credit card can vary on the issuing bank or the program for which you are applying.

Sage Advice: The differences in interest rates, how your monthly balance is computed, and annual fees can be substantial so shop wisely.

6. If you are short of cash, consider tapping your credit cards for cash advances, which give you access to instant cash.

Sage Advice: Be careful about using cash advance too freely. In addition to interest that usually begins to accumulate as soon as the advance is made, loan fees are charged.

7. Know the difference between Credit Cards and Debit Cards. Debit Cards look like credit cards, but instead of sending you bills to be paid later, a debit card immediately deducts the required payment from your savings/checking account.

Sage Advice: Monitor your use of debit cards carefully, as purchases decrease your account balance that day. Enter debit card transactions into your register immediately, just as you would ATM withdrawals or checks you write.

8. Bank Rate Monitor will provide you information about low interest rate credit cards. Call them at (407) 627-7330 for more information.

Sage Advice: Don't just apply to the first credit card application you receive. Compare several cards to determine which is right for you.

9. Signs that you are suffering from credit carditis:

- Your credit cards are always at their limits.
- You use the maximum credit each month on more than three credit cards at a time.
- You fall behind on other monthly bills, such as mortgages, car loans, etc. to pay your credit cards.
- You show people your credit card when they ask to see a picture of your kids.

Sage Advice: Track your credit card balance like you would a bank account and don't go higher than you can pay off in one or two months.

10. If you are totally out of control, contact some non-profit organizations to help you through your credit problems.

Sage Advice: One of the best organizations is the National Foundation for Consumer Credit. They can be reached at (800) 388-2227

11. See our Bonus Interactive Credit Card Worksheet to determine how much interest you're REALLY paying every month.

APPENDIX 10

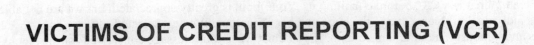

VICTIMS OF CREDIT REPORTING (VCR)

Victims of Credit Reporting (VCR)

http://members.aol.com/davevest/vcr.html.

A place to learn about credit reports and what we can do about them

- <u>What is VCR</u>
  A brief discussion about VCR and our views
- <u>Can You Believe It?</u>
  Current schemes to make your life impossible
- <u>Not So Current Events</u>
  Events from the recent past
- <u>Your Nosey Boss</u> and <u>You'll Never Know</u>
  Employment Discrimination and Credit Reports
- <u>Changes</u>
  Legal Changes We Propose
- <u>The Players</u>
  Links to Credit Agencies and other players

<u>Email Received</u>
<u>Credit Scoring</u>
Cream Skimmers and Pigeon Guts
<u>Credit Repair</u>
How to be victimized twice by one credit report
<u>U.S. Consumer Credit Laws</u>
<u>European Law</u>
Compare this with the lobbyist written law above, which protects only corporations
<u>Links</u>
Interesting links that we are looking at
<u>Mellow Out!</u>
A lighter Look at Privacy

Coming This Summer: A faster mirror site and a virtual tour thru the *Avenging Angel* Credit Bureau!

We are always glad to hear from those who agree with us, and frequently learn from those who don't. Keep the email coming. We have an ongoing need for examples of problems caused by medical providers and insurance companies.

Please read "What is VCR" before e-mailing us. Your input is greatly appreciated, but we are not able to address individual problems due to the huge number of victims. We post selected e-mails anonymously in our letters column. If you don't want your message considered for this, let us know. Be patient--our staff is limited and mostly volunteer.

E-mail MUST have the word VCR in the subject line.

You can find the e-mail address for your US Representative by clicking here <u>House</u>

You can find the e-mail address for your US Senator by clicking here <u>Senate</u>

Anybody out there? Give us some feedback! <u>Send VCR mail</u>

Current Happenings to Fret About

Companies Screwing Up Your Credit Because You Pay *On Time*

If you think you couldn't possibly be blacklisted because you always pay quickly, think again. GE is the latest firm to consider you a deadbeat for **not** paying late. When any card is cancelled because you didn't incur late fees or interest, it shows up on your credit report as "closed by the creditor". At that point scoring systems brand you as unworthy to enter a pay toilet, let alone get another card. **More info:** The New Deadbeats

"A little *solvent* to be applying for a SEARS card, aren't you?"

SEARS has recently been declining debt free applicants with clean credit records in their 40s for "Age Grouping". The victims can't find what nefarious scoring practice this phrase refers to, but it likely means that *good* customers that age should have at least 10 thousand in credit card debt and a few glitches on their credit record. *Our Translation: Sears wants only customers who have debt problems so they can collect late charges.* (It is well known this is the case with many banks.) As if to prove our point, Sears just blew $165 million to settle charges that they were making deals with those already in bankruptcy so they could go right from the courthouse and rack up more debt on their SEARS card. Now we know what they mean by *"Come see the softer side of Sears!"*

Protect Your Mail --- Lose Your Credit

June 1993 Several members throughout the country are reporting the sudden inability to get credit after opening Post Office Boxes on the advice of postal officials and law enforcement. Mail theft is an increasing problem in urban areas, where residents of many neighborhoods are advised to have mail sent to PO boxes to avoid having it stolen. The credit bureaus promptly use lists supplied by your US Post Office, including private PO Box street addresses, to put boxholders on "fraud alert". Understand that it is not the use of a box in applying for credit that gets you blacklisted, but the mere possession of a box even if not listed on the loan application. This "special" designation (or the outdated/erroneous addresses and their sources) seldom show up on *your* copy of the report, but results in application rejection. Reason for rejection is usually listed as "past delinquent accounts". **May '97 Update** - The mail privacy situation has gotten much worse. Experian is now retaining address and PO Box records permanently. Reports obtained in May 1997 are showing PO Box addresses from 18 years ago--including several which were obtained from magazine subscription databases and at least one political campaign. Experian is the only bureau honest enough to at least show the erroneous data to victims, but we have never seen as blatant a violation of the 7 year rule, especially since the reports often show the source as a collection agency. Credit scoring systems can scour these ancient addresses (and who reported them) for any evidence of debt well over the legal reporting time and presto, "past delinquent accounts" haunt you from the Johnson administration. You can complain to the bureaus by writing to them at their own PO Boxes.

Congress Exempts Bureaus From Privacy Laws

Public comments to the FTC on pending database privacy laws are in and available on the web. Catching us by surprise was a mention in the response by VISA/MASTERCARD that Congress has exempted credit bureaus from the law right from the start. Congress either just doesn't get it or is trying to redirect citizen anger to online phone books and away from their luncheon buddies at the credit bureaus. Kudos to the FTC for putting the comments on the web. It helps balance out the pro bureau pages mentioned below.

FTC Toes the Company Line

The Federal Trade Commission has put up a new bunch of web pages that are so anti-victim you have to hold your nose to read them. The FTCs weak apologies for allowing clearly discriminatory practices is illuminating.

(Did you know that it is not age discrimination to treat everyone ages 30 to 50 as though they have massive debt, regardless of the actual debt of the individual?) Co-sponsored by two extremely pro-banker groups, it appears the pages were written to deflect consumer demands that change occur in credit evaluation practices. (The FTC has failed to bring criminal charges against a single person in the credit bureau racket, despite huge numbers of complaints.) The web site is worth reading, if only to see how credit bureau marketing fantasies are repeated as fact. Face it folks, this watchdog is just a butler to the industry.

Equifax Accused Of Selling Voting Records To Bill Collectors

A recently acquired subsidiary of Equifax (CDB-California Data Bureau) faces a private lawsuit over the illegal sale of voting records to skip tracers and bill collectors, reports *Businesswire*. (California's Attorney General was apparently too busy taping commercials for the credit bureaus to handle this.) The same firm was caught selling social security and voter information in Arizona in 1995 and was subject to a 1993 consent decree which was apparently filed in a drawer and forgotten. This is so outrageous even Equifax shareholders demanded an explanation.

Car Rental Companies do it to Victims yet again

The rental car industry has made life miserable for Credit Report Victims for some time. Now it appears some AVIS dealers routinely discriminated against black and Jewish customers. Avis, which is owned by the same conglomerate that owns Days Inn and Century 21, claims to have revoked the problem franchise. In other car rental news, Avis and Hertz raised their noses to the ceiling and said they do not wish to deal with customers who have debit, as opposed to credit cards. This was opposed by MasterCard and VISA. Debit cards are frequently used by those who dislike debt or have had their lives messed up by credit reports. **Secured credit cards are likely to be refused next.** Incredibly, some "consumer groups" approved the move. More from CNN.

Utilities Quietly giving your address to Credit Bureaus

US West is just one major utility that now blabs your personal data to credit bureaus when you first apply for service, usually without telling you. In most countries the phone company reports your application to the local identity registration officials, who keep the info private. Here your name, new address, employer and anything else they can get out of you are given to credit bureaus who sell it to anyone who pays. The end result? The German has privacy and quiet. But your phone rings and salesman knock at your door before you even move in. In other communication news, naive politicians and police agencies (LAPD again!) have been caught encouraging beeper companies and landlords to decline those with even a tiny blemish on the theory that credit reports predict criminal tendencies.

Thieves and Credit Agencies Team Up To Punish Victims

An ongoing fad in the credit reporting/scoring industry is to treat those who have debit/credit cards stolen as if they themselves are thieves. Credit bureaus now report the theft of a card on your report, and it is often scored in the same way as a major loan default. Ready for the next step? Odds are good that within the next year other types of crimes will be used against the victim and credit bureaus will call it a public service! *("I'm sorry ma'am, but our other patrons would be uncomfortable with a rape victim eating next to them.")* Thanks to the civic minded folks at credit bureaus, you are now forced to decide between reporting a crime to police and losing the ability to conduct business for seven years. **So think carefully before you use that toll free number to report a stolen card--it may be better to just close the account without explanation.**
VCR Homepage

CREDIT SCORING

The update on this page has taken so long it's time we stopped promising. Not to worry though! Bayhouse covers the topic with much gusto. If you live in a library, look for recent articles by Kenneth Harney in the Washington Post.

CREDIT SCORING –

Fannie Mae and Freddie Mac (Federal Agencies with vast influence over lending policies) have decreed that all mortgages with Federal connections in the United States must use credit scoring to evaluate applicants by late 1996.

The credit scoring procedure is an automated evaluation tool used to evaluate both credit applications AND risk in existing credit lines. The procedure is completely hidden from applicants and there are no effective Federal controls that limit what can and cannot be evaluated by a computerized system using credit scoring.

Credit Scoring is not a new concept. Stock brokers in the sixties and seventies originally developed mathematical formulas designed to predict which stocks would rise in value based on a stew of information contained in public and private records. Several firms boldly predicated that their computers could outplay the stock market and make billionaires of those who used their systems. But, as with any attempt to predict the future, the programs failed miserably when fairly evaluated by outside analysis and were largely abandoned when reports surfaced that showed computerized performance predictions fared worse that random guesses on the stock market. Wall Street still considers predictive programs to be a huge flop and the purveyors of this financial snake oil have to look elsewhere to sell their products.

Now the computer gurus are back (after a short stint selling programs to predict pony races at the track), and this time they have sold their crystal ball promises to Federal regulators who apparently have no memory of the earlier failed experiments. And guess who suffers - You and I and the economy of any country foolish enough to bet everything on computerized fortune tellers,

How does credit scoring supposedly work? Your daily transactions are followed by computers at "service provider" centers. The ongoing evaluation process looks at credit balances, purchases, address changes and a variety of questionable data items that are not part of your credit report. What they look at varies institution by institution. Some look at positively weird things like birth weight and your kids school grades (both provided by the Department of Education)), but most include such usual items as deposits, credit card purchases and debt ratios.

And what has our Government done to protect us? Even though credit reports have been the number one consumer complaint for 5 years running, Congress has seen no need to enact legislation to protect the public from losing credit, insurance, homes and jobs for actions over which they had little control. Just recently the Federal Trade Commission threw up its hands in surrender and declared that Congress had failed to update the Fair Credit Reporting Act sufficiently to allow the agency jurisdiction over credit scoring. FTC Press Release

As it stands now victims of this scheme do not even have the right to know if they were denied credit by a machine or a human, let alone review or challenge the scores involved. Industry publications estimate over *85* percent of all consumer credit granting decisions are made by computer. With the new Federal regulations requiring it, that number will hit 99% in no time. And congress grants no protection at all to victims of credit scoring, insisting that you can "fix" credit reporting problems by attaching a cute little note to a credit file that will never be seen by human eyes. Thousands of American victims can only reply "Yah Right".

How can we protect themselves? *We can't.* At this time US citizens have no real protection, but that doesn't mean it can't be done. Most democracies including the Netherlands have essentially outlawed credit reports as Americans know them since the 1970's, and have thriving economies. In fact, countries that have outlawed blacklists (i.e. credit reports) have managed to end up owning a huge share of our banks. For the time being, we are the only country without meaningful protection against credit reports and "ghost scoring" (Canada plays a close second).

APPENDIX 11

12 CREDIT CARD SECRETS

12 CREDIT CARD SECRETS

Banks Don't Want You to Know

This pamphlet is a publication of the <u>Executive Offices of Consumer Affairs.</u> and contains a summary of your rights as a tenant. For further information:

Massachusetts Executive Office of Consumer Affairs and Business Regulation 1 Ashburton Place Boston, Massachusetts 02108 (617) 727-7780

1. **INTEREST BACKDATING**

   Most card issuers charge interest from the day a charge is posted to your account if you don't pay in full monthly. But, some charge interest from the date of purchase, days before they have even paid the store on your behalf!

   REMEDY: Find another card issuer, or always pay your bill in full by the due date.

2. **TWO-CYCLE BILLING**

   Issuers which use this method of calculating interest, charge two months worth of interest for the first month you failed to pay off your total balance in full. This issue arises only when you switch from paying in full to carrying a balance from month to month.

   REMEDY: Switch issuers or always pay your balance in full.

3. **THE RIGHT TO SETOFF**

   If you have money on deposit at a bank, and also have your credit card there, you may have signed an agreement when you opened the deposit account which permits the bank to take those funds if you become delinquent on your credit card.

   REMEDY: Bank at separate institutions, or avoid delinquencies.

4. **FEES ARE NEGOTIABLE**

   You may be paying up to $50 a year or more as an annual fee on your credit card. You may also be subject to finance charges of over 18%.

   REMEDY: If you are a good customer, the bank may be willing to drop the annual fee, and reduce the interest rate -- you only have to ask! Otherwise, you can switch issuers to a lower- priced card.

5. **INTEREST RATE HIKES ARE RETROACTIVE**

   If you sign up for a credit card with a low "teaser" rate, such as 7.9%, when the low rate period expires, your existing balance will likely be subject to the regular and substantially higher interest rate.

   REMEDY: Pay in full before the rate increase or close the account.

6. **SHORTENED DUE DATES**
   Most card issuers offer a 25 day grace period in which to pay for new purchases without incurring finance charges. Some banks have shortened the grace period to 20 days--but only for customers who pay in full monthly.

   REMEDY: Ask to go back to 25 days.

7. **ELIMINATING GRACE PERIODS**
   That fabulous offer you received in the mail for a gold card with a $10,000 credit limit, and lots of features may not be so great. The most common "string" attached is the card has no grace period. You are charged interest on everything from the day you buy it, even if you pay on time.

   REMEDY: Throw the offer out!

8. **DISAPPEARING BENEFITS**
   Many banks enticed you to sign up with extra benefits such as lifetime warranty, a 5% discount on all travel, or protection if an item purchased is lost. Now, some banks have cut back on these extras without the fanfare that launched them.

   REMEDY: Read annual disclosure of changes, and switch cards if need be.

9. **DOUBLE FEES ON CASH ADVANCES**
   Most credit cards impose both finance charges and a transaction fee on cash advances. Interest starts from the day of the advance, and the transaction fee can be up to 2.5% of the amount taken. Beware of cards advertising "no finance charges." Transaction fees may still apply.

   REMEDY: Limit cash advances.

10. **FEWER RIGHTS ON DEBIT CARDS**
    Some Visa and MasterCards have payments deducted directly from your checking account (debit cards). Under Federal law, you technically don't have the same right to "charge back" problem purchases as you do with a conventional credit card. Also, if the card is lost or stolen, you can have up to unlimited liability for losses if you don't report the problem within 60 days, which is different from the $50 maximum liability on credit cards. (Exception: the $50 limit applies to debit cards as well as to credit cards in Massachusetts.)

    REMEDY: Know your card. Is it a credit card or debit card? They can look alike.

11. **MISLEADING MONTHLY MINIMUMS**
    You may think it is beneficial to have a card where you only need to pay 2%-3% of your balance monthly. It is just the opposite. The bank stands to make far more money from finance charges the longer you carry out payments--and you foot the bill.

    REMEDY: Pay all you can monthly.

12. **INTEREST FROM DAY ONE**
    When you carry a balance from month to month, there is no grace period on new purchases on most cards. The 20-25 day grace period where no finance charges accrue does not apply when you don't pay in full each month.

    REMEDY: Find cards that exclude new purchases when calculating interest.

APPENDIX 12

▽

TRANS UNION CREDIT REPORT

1. Your Trans Union subscriber inquiry code number.

2. Market and sub-market area in which the credit file resides. An asterisk (*) indicates additional identifying information has been added since the last cycle.

3. How long the consumer has been in the credit bureau files.

4. Date and time the credit report was issued.

5. Consumer's name and alias, if any.

6. Consumer's social security number. An asterisk (*) indicates the social security number was on the credit file before your access.

7. Consumer's date of birth.

8. Consumers complete address and the date the address was first reported TO THE CREDIT BUREAU

9. Consumers home phone number.

10. Consumer's previous address and the date reported.

11. Consumer's second previous address and dale reported.

12. Spouse's name and social security number.

13. Consumer's employer and address

14. Consumer's position and income.

15. Employment dales hired (H) and terminated.

16. Date reported (R) or verified (V) by the bureau.

17. Previous employer and address.

18. Previous position and income.

19. Dates consumer was hired (H) and terminated (I) at former place of employment.

20. Date employment was reported (R) or verified (V).

21. Spouse's complete employment, company name, address, position, and dates hired (H), terminated), reported (R) or verified (V).

22. Summary: Total number of accounts (TRD), total negative accounts (NEG), total number of public records (PUB), total number of collection sets (COL), total number of inquiries (INO), cumulative balance on all accounts (BAL), high credit-credit limits on accounts showing both high credit and credit limit (HC-CL).

22. Delphi scores and factors, trans-alert and hawk messages. NOTE: Actual messages appear at end of credit report.

24. Name and number of reporting subscriber.

25. Date account opened.

26. The high credit on the account (the highest amount ever owed).

27. The date verified, month and year followed by one alpha character. The alpha character defines the meaning of the date (refer to date indicators tables).

28. Balance owing as of the date in date verified field.

29. Type of account:
    R = revolving
    I = installment
    O = open 30.60 or 90 day account
    C = check credit
    M = mortgage
    The ACB manner of payment rat-mg system (see mop table)

30. Terms: Number of payments, payment frequency and dollar amount due each payment. The codes are
    X = unspecified
    M = monthly
    P = payroll deduction
    S = semiannual
    O = quarterly
    Y = yearly
    W = weekly
    B = bimonthly
    MIN = minimum

31. Date account closed, month and year followed by one alpha character. The alpha character defines the meaning of the date (refer to date indicators table).

32. Responsibility for repaying this debt (i.e. individual account, authorized user account, etc. Refer to ECCA inquiry and account designators table).

33. Type of loan.

34. Payment pattern with actual manner of payment ratings 1 through 5 for maximum of 24 months. It reads from left to right with the most current verified entry on the left. An X is used when no rating is available or the rating is not I -5, for example, unrated, zero, UC or too new to rate. The first entry corresponds to the date in the date verified column.

35. Credit limit: the maximum amount of credit approved by the creditor.

36. Maximum delinquency consists of three columns: the date the maximum state of delinquency occurred, the dollar amount and the rating at the time of the delinquency.

37. Historical status displays in four columns: A V- indicates that the credit grantor has provided the counters for the number of months the account is under review. The first column is for the number of months the credit grantor is reviewing the account, the second, third and fourth columns indicate the number of times the consumer has been over 30 days, over 60 days and over 90 days late on the account.

38. The collateral for an installment loan.

39. Remarks column is used if the account is in some type of dispute or requires an explanation of the credit condition of the account.

40. This position shows the inquiries made on a consumer's credit file. 11 four or more inquiries are made on a consumer in less than 60 days a trans-alert warning will appear on the report. The first number listed indicates the total number of inquiries posted. The inquiry field shows the date of the inquiry, the ECOA designator, subscriber inquiry code and sub- scriber name. The loan type and loan amount (if applicable), are given after the subscriber name.

41. Public record information will be listed on the credit file (if applicable). Included in the public record information is the location of the court where the public record was recorded, the court type, the date the public record was reported to the bureau, the ECCA designator, any liabilities or assets and the type of public record. Also listed will be the date paid (if applicable), the docket number, the plaintiff and attorney involved in the case.

42. A consumer statement may appear here.

43. Trans-alert message.

44. Hawk-alert message.

45. Indicates the end of the last page of credit report.

46. Identification of the bureau owning the credit file

KINDS OF BUSINESS CLASSIFICATION

A   Automotive
B   Bank:
C   Clothing
D   Department and Variety
F   Finance
G   Groceries
H   Home Furnishings
I   Insurance
J   Jewelry and Cameras
K   Contractor:
L   Lumber Building Material, Hardware
M   Medical and Related Health
N   National Credit Card
O   Oil and National Credit Card Companies
P   Personal Services Other Than Medical
Q   Mail Order Houses
R   Real Estate and Public Accommodations:
S   Sporting Goods
T   Farm and Garden Supplies
U   Utilities and Fuel
V   Government
W   Wholesale
X   Advertising
V   Collection Services
Z   Miscellaneous

MANNER OF PAYMENT CODES

00 = TOO new to rate or approve, but not used.
01 = Pays within 30 days of billing.
02 = Pays in more than 30 days, but not more than 60 days. Currently 1 payment past due.
03 = Pays in more than 60 days, but not more than 90 days. Currently 2 payments past due.
04 = Pays in more than 9O days, but not more than 120 days. Currently 3 payments past due.
O5 = Pays in more than 120 days. Currently 3 or more payments   past due.
07 = Making regular payments under wage earner plan or similar arrangement.
O8 = Repossession
8A = Voluntary repossession
8D = Legal repossession
8P = Payment to a repossession account
8R = Repossession redeemed
09 = Bad debt; charged-off account; Profit & loss account
9B = Collection account: Attorney account
9P = Payment to a charged-off or collection account
UR = Unrated
UC = Unclassified
RJ = Rejected

DATE INDICATORS

A   Automated
C- Closed
D   Declined
F   Repossessed / written off / collection
H   Hired
I   Indirect
M   Manually frozen
N   No record
P   Paid out
R   Reported but not verified
S   Slow answering
T   Terminated or frozen
V   Verified
X   No reply

ECOA INQUIRY AND ACCOUNT DESIGNATORS

A   Authorized user of shared account
C   Joint contractual liability
I   Individual account for sole use of applicant
M   Co-signer primarily liable for account
N   Non-applicant spouse inquiry
P   Participant in shared account which cannot be distinguished as C or A
S   Co-signer, no spousal relationship
T   Relationship with account terminated
U   Undesignated

PAYMENT PATTERN

X   Not reported by subscriber
1   On time
2   30 days late
3   60 days late
4   90 days late
5   120 or more days late
P   Reduction to balance on account with MOP greater than 05
N   No reduction to balance on account with MOP greater than 05

EXAMPLE OF PAYMENT PATTERN:

Trade line has a verification date of 4188 and mop is 9P.
The payment pattern is as follows:

(4/88)	(3188)	(2J%8)	(1188)	(12187)	(1 ¶187)	(I O~87)	(9~S7)	(8187)	(7187)	(6187)	(5/8)
P	P	N	N	P	P	P	5	4	3	2	1
I	I	I	1	1	1	1	1	1	1	1	1
(4/87)	(3/87)	(2/87)	(1/87)	(12/86)	(11/86)	(10/86)	(9/86)	(8/86)	(7/86)	(6/86)	(5/86)

4/88:   A payment was received on the profit & loss/collection account
3/88:   A payment was received on the account
2/88:   NO payment was received on the account.
1/88:   NO payment was received on the account.
12/87:   A payment was received.
11/87:   A payment was received.
10/87:   A payment was received.
9/87:   The account was 120 or more days behind.
8/87:   The account was 90 days behind.
7/87:   The account was 60 days behind.
6/87:   The account was 30 days behind.
5/87:   The account was current.
4/87 through 5/86:   The account was: current.

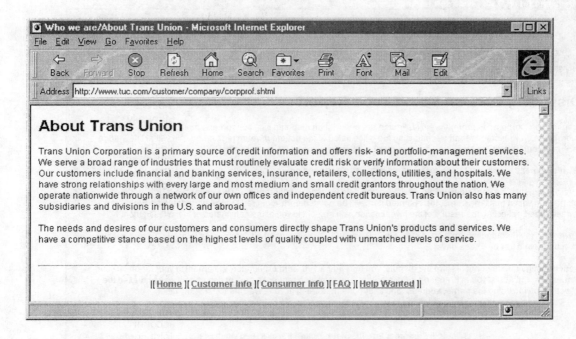

About Trans Union

Trans Union Corporation is a primary source of credit information and offers risk- and portfolio-management services. We serve a broad range of industries that must routinely evaluate credit risk or verify information about their customers. Our customers include financial and banking services, insurance, retailers, collections, utilities, and hospitals. We have strong relationships with every large and most medium and small credit grantors throughout the nation. We operate nationwide through a network of our own offices and independent credit bureaus. Trans Union also has many subsidiaries and divisions in the U.S. and abroad.

The needs and desires of our customers and consumers directly shape Trans Union's products and services. We have a competitive stance based on the highest levels of quality coupled with unmatched levels of service.

|[Home][Customer Info][Consumer Info][FAQ][Help Wanted]|

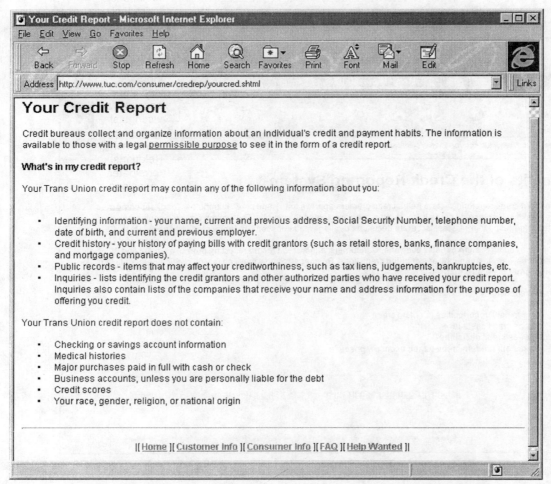

Your Credit Report

Credit bureaus collect and organize information about an individual's credit and payment habits. The information is available to those with a legal permissible purpose to see it in the form of a credit report.

What's in my credit report?

Your Trans Union credit report may contain any of the following information about you:

- Identifying information - your name, current and previous address, Social Security Number, telephone number, date of birth, and current and previous employer.
- Credit history - your history of paying bills with credit grantors (such as retail stores, banks, finance companies, and mortgage companies).
- Public records - items that may affect your creditworthiness, such as tax liens, judgements, bankruptcies, etc.
- Inquiries - lists identifying the credit grantors and other authorized parties who have received your credit report. Inquiries also contain lists of the companies that receive your name and address information for the purpose of offering you credit.

Your Trans Union credit report does not contain:

- Checking or savings account information
- Medical histories
- Major purchases paid in full with cash or check
- Business accounts, unless you are personally liable for the debt
- Credit scores
- Your race, gender, religion, or national origin

|[Home][Customer Info][Consumer Info][FAQ][Help Wanted]|

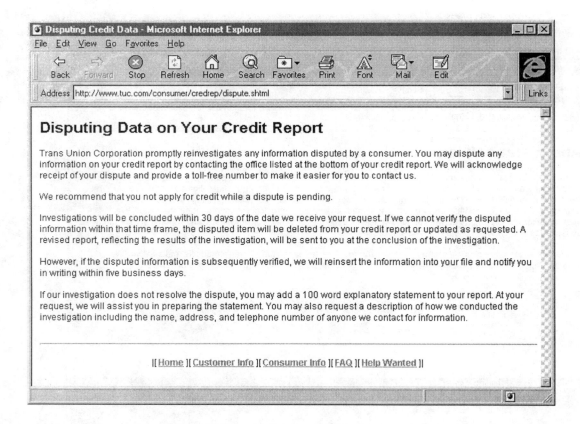

Disputing Data on Your Credit Report

Trans Union Corporation promptly reinvestigates any information disputed by a consumer. You may dispute any information on your credit report by contacting the office listed at the bottom of your credit report. We will acknowledge receipt of your dispute and provide a toll-free number to make it easier for you to contact us.

We recommend that you not apply for credit while a dispute is pending.

Investigations will be concluded within 30 days of the date we receive your request. If we cannot verify the disputed information within that time frame, the disputed item will be deleted from your credit report or updated as requested. A revised report, reflecting the results of the investigation, will be sent to you at the conclusion of the investigation.

However, if the disputed information is subsequently verified, we will reinsert the information into your file and notify you in writing within five business days.

If our investigation does not resolve the dispute, you may add a 100 word explanatory statement to your report. At your request, we will assist you in preparing the statement. You may also request a description of how we conducted the investigation including the name, address, and telephone number of anyone we contact for information.

|[Home][Customer Info][Consumer Info][FAQ][Help Wanted]|

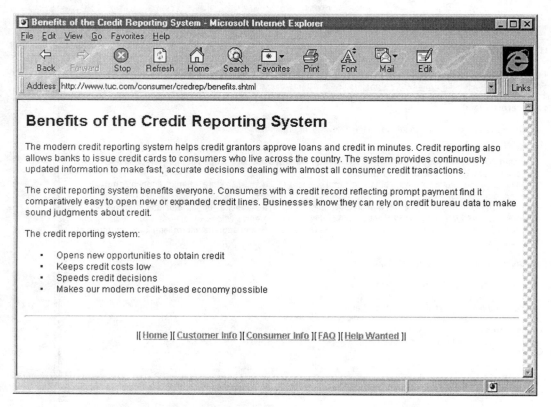

Benefits of the Credit Reporting System

The modern credit reporting system helps credit grantors approve loans and credit in minutes. Credit reporting also allows banks to issue credit cards to consumers who live across the country. The system provides continuously updated information to make fast, accurate decisions dealing with almost all consumer credit transactions.

The credit reporting system benefits everyone. Consumers with a credit record reflecting prompt payment find it comparatively easy to open new or expanded credit lines. Businesses know they can rely on credit bureau data to make sound judgments about credit.

The credit reporting system:

- Opens new opportunities to obtain credit
- Keeps credit costs low
- Speeds credit decisions
- Makes our modern credit-based economy possible

|[Home][Customer Info][Consumer Info][FAQ][Help Wanted]|

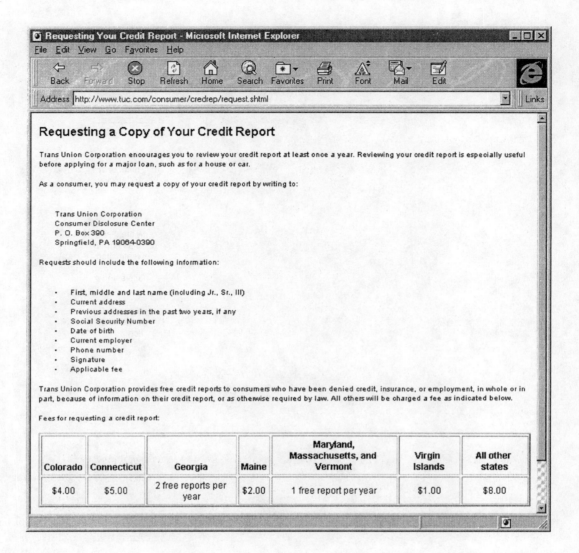

Requesting a Copy of Your Credit Report

Trans Union Corporation encourages you to review your credit report at least once a year. Reviewing your credit report is especially useful before applying for a major loan, such as for a house or car.

As a consumer, you may request a copy of your credit report by writing to:

Trans Union Corporation
Consumer Disclosure Center
P. O. Box 390
Springfield, PA 19064-0390

Requests should include the following information:

- First, middle and last name (including Jr., Sr., III)
- Current address
- Previous addresses in the past two years, if any
- Social Security Number
- Date of birth
- Current employer
- Phone number
- Signature
- Applicable fee

Trans Union Corporation provides free credit reports to consumers who have been denied credit, insurance, or employment, in whole or in part, because of information on their credit report, or as otherwise required by law. All others will be charged a fee as indicated below.

Fees for requesting a credit report:

Colorado	Connecticut	Georgia	Maine	Maryland, Massachusetts, and Vermont	Virgin Islands	All other states
$4.00	$5.00	2 free reports per year	$2.00	1 free report per year	$1.00	$8.00

INDEX

- A -

alias, 22, 200
automobile dealer, 86
automobile loan, 16

- B -

bad credit, 7, 8, 22, 29, 31, 51, 53, 67, 83
balance transfer, 103
Bank Rate Monitor™, 92, 94
bankruptcy, 19, 23, 34, 48, 49, 73, 74, 101, 102, 103, 131, 133, 134, 137, 153, 178, 180, 189

- C -

CCV, 80
check authorization service, 78
check verification service, 78, 79
collection agency, 20, 44, 45, 124, 151, 160, 189
college student, 67
confidential credit, 107, 108
consolidation loan, 73, 74
consumer protection agencies, 78
credit bureau, 8, 10, 11, 17, 18, 19, 20, 21, 22, 23, 24, 28, 29, 30, 31, 35, 36, 39, 40, 41, 42, 43, 45, 46, 47, 48, 49, 52, 53, 54, 55, 56, 57, 58, 66, 68, 69, 73, 77, 79, 82, 83, 85, 86, 87, 103, 108, 109, 159, 160, 184, 190, 200
credit card, 8, 10, 11, 13, 15, 16, 19, 21, 23, 28, 34, 35, 36, 38, 58, 62, 63, 65, 66, 67, 68, 69, 72, 73, 74, 78, 90, 92, 93, 101, 102, 103, 104, 105, 119, 131, 147, 148, 152, 153, 183, 184, 185, 189, 191, 195, 196, 197
credit clinics, 30, 31
credit culture, 11, 19, 61, 62
credit, good, 7, 8, 18, 31, 36, 61, 66, 92, 104, 132, 184
credit, no, 8, 15, 31, 33, 36, 58, 110
credit grantor, 10, 11, 13, 18, 108, 109, 112, 139, 201

credit history, 10, 19, 20, 21, 22, 23, 24, 31, 33, 34, 35, 36, 38, 44, 46, 48, 51, 53, 54, 55, 56, 57, 58, 63, 66, 67, 68, 71, 81, 82, 86, 104, 130, 131, 132, 136, 184
credit, preapproved, 64, 65, 66, 67, 92, 147

- D -

danger zone, 23
dispute procedure, 38

- E -

Equifax, 18, 30, 94, 173, 174, 177, 179, 180, 184, 190
Experian, 18, 29, 107, 109, 130, 131, 132, 133, 134, 189

- F -

Fair Credit Reporting Act, 24, 27, 28, 29, 30, 31, 37, 38, 39, 40, 42, 43, 77, 79, 82, 92, 110, 119, 139, 173, 192
Federal Archive, 48, 49
Federal Bankruptcy Court, 21
Federal Government, 65
Federal Trade Commission, or FTC, 28, 39, 40, 41, 42, 81, 82, 86, 126, 148, 149, 189, 190, 192
fictitious name, 87
file segregation, 55
financial hardship, 71, 79
fixed monthly expenses, 72
frivolous dispute, 109

- I -

identification reports, 82
individual financial institution, 14
information brokers, 82, 86, 109, 110
injunctive relief, 45, 108

inquiry, 21, 37, 42, 56, 68, 87, 104, 132, 136, 137, 138, 165, 173, 181, 200, 201, 202
installment loan, 16
Interbank Association, 14, 78
Internet, 31, 91, 92, 93, 94, 95, 96, 97, 98, 147, 149
investigative credit report, 24, 89, 90

- J -

junk mail, 66

- M -

mortgage loan, 16

- N -

nonpayment, 44, 78

- P -

portable loan, 16
proprietary card, 15
public record information, 21, 46, 48, 49, 55, 56, 124, 137, 139, 201

- R -

real estate agent, 86
residential landlord, 86
revolving credit, 14, 23, 136

- S -

Sage advice, 184, 185
scam, 35, 86, 91, 92, 149
SCAN, 80
Small Claims Court, 28, 43, 45, 108
Social Security Number, 2, 10, 20, 22, 30, 48, 53, 56, 57, 58, 66, 79, 80, 82, 136, 138, 164, 165, 166, 175

- T -

Telecheck, 80
Trans Union Corporation, 18, 30
Travel and entertainment card, 15

- W -

warning programs, 22, 46, 49, 51, 52, 53, 55, 57, 68, 83, 87, 88